REVISE PEARSON EDEXCEL GCSE (9–1) Physics

GRADES 7–9 Revision & Practice

Series consultant: Harry Smith
Authors: Helen Sayers and Jim Newall

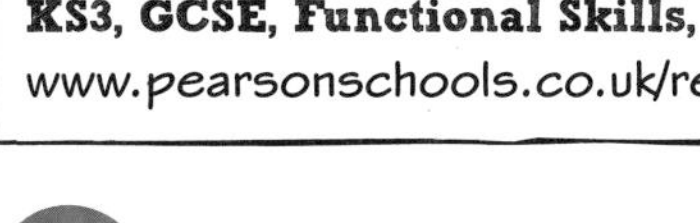

Contents

Use this quick quiz to check that you are confident with the core skills and knowledge you need for the Pearson Edexcel GCSE (9–1) Physics Higher exam or Combined Science Higher exam.

Check your understanding with solutions to all the exam-style questions.

A small bit of small print

Pearson Edexcel publishes Sample Assessment Material and the Specification on its website. This is the official content and this book should be used in conjunction with it. The questions in the *Exam practice* sections have been written to help you revise topics and practise answering exam questions. Remember – the real exam questions may not look like this.

Welcome to Nail it!

This book provides revision and practice to help you nail down a top grade in your Pearson Edexcel GCSE (9–1) Physics Higher exam or Combined Science Higher exam. Designed for students aiming for a grade 7, 8 or 9, it's packed with exam tips, support for tricky topics, and exam-style practice questions to make sure you are ready to tackle the toughest questions and achieve top marks.

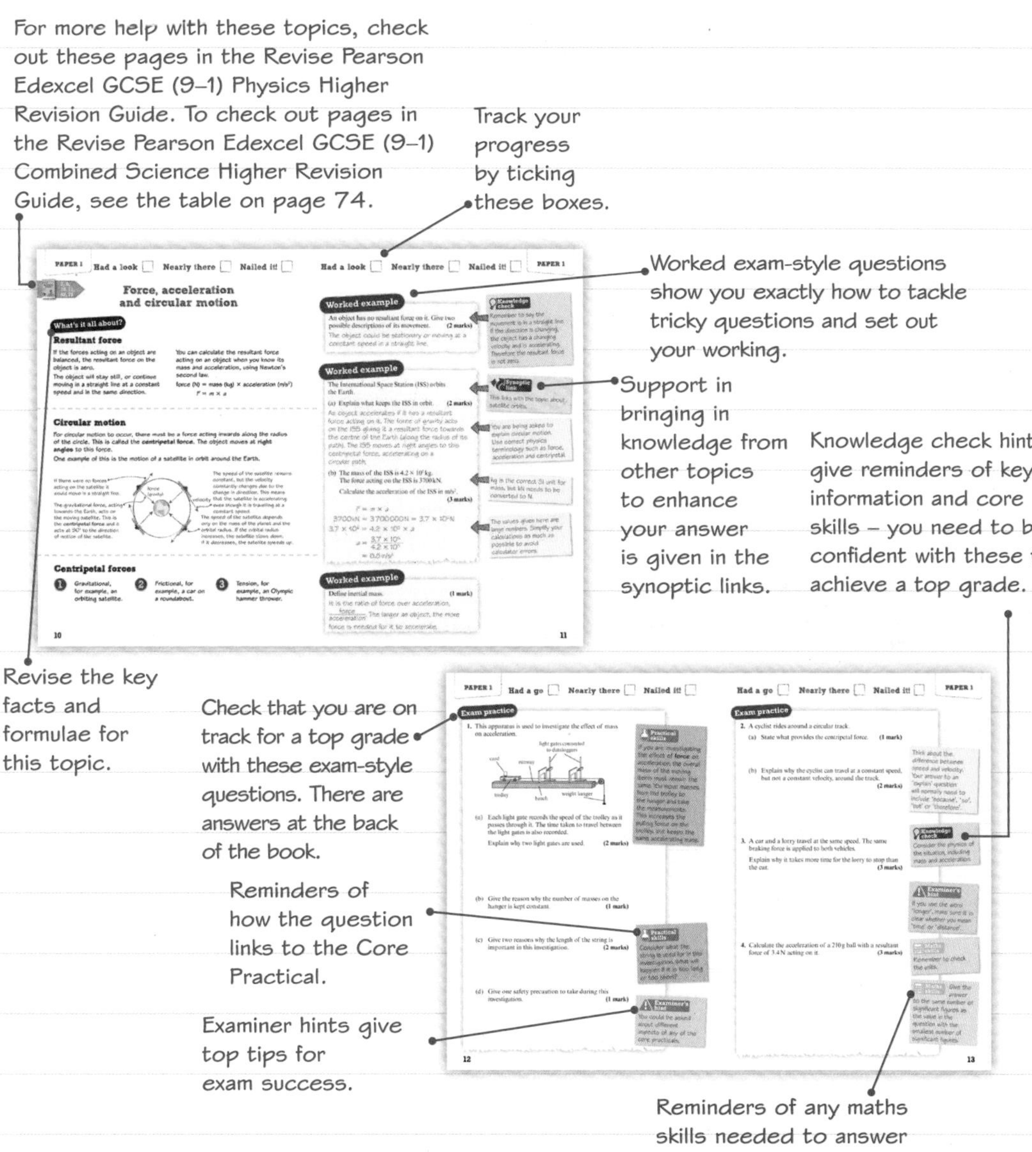

Knowledge check

If you're aiming for a top grade, you need to be confident with core skills and knowledge, such as acceleration, electrical circuits and sound waves. Take this quick quiz to find out which skills you might need to brush up on before tackling the topics in this book. Answers are on page 66.

Revise core skills

Use the **Revise Pearson Edexcel GCSE (9–1) Physics Higher Revision Guide** if you need to revise any of the core skills. The green arrow next to each question tells you which page to look at for more help.

6 **1.** What is the acceleration, *g*, in free fall?

- ☐ **A** 0.1 m/s^2
- ☐ **B** 1 m/s^2
- ☐ **C** 10 m/s^2
- ☐ **D** 100 m/s^2

6 **2.** What is the typical speed of a cyclist?

- ☐ **A** 1 m/s
- ☐ **B** 2.5 m/s
- ☐ **C** 6 m/s
- ☐ **D** 15 m/s

5 **3.** What is the formula to calculate the area of a right-angled triangle with base *b* and height *h*?

- ☐ **A** $0.5 \times b \times h$
- ☐ **B** $(b \times h)^2$
- ☐ **C** $2 \times b \times h$
- ☐ **D** $0.5\,(b \times h)^2$

8 **4.** Define Newton's second law.

....

....

5. What is the weight of an object with mass 2.5 kg?

- ☐ **A** 0.25 N
- ☐ **B** 2.5 N
- ☐ **C** 25 N
- ☐ **D** 250 N

6. What is the momentum of an object with a mass of 5 kg travelling at 15 m/s?

- ☐ **A** 0.3 kg m/s
- ☐ **B** 3 kg m/s
- ☐ **C** 75 kg m/s
- ☐ **D** 1125 kg m/s

7. Which equation is correct?

- ☐ **A** braking distance = thinking distance + stopping distance
- ☐ **B** stopping distance = thinking distance + braking distance
- ☐ **C** thinking distance = braking distance + stopping distance
- ☐ **D** stopping distance = braking distance – thinking distance

8. What type of wave is a sound wave?

9. What is the formula for frequency?

- [ ] **A** wavelength ÷ wave speed
- [ ] **B** wave speed ÷ wavelength
- [ ] **C** wave speed × wavelength
- [ ] **D** wave speed^2 × wavelength

10. What type of sound waves are used to destroy kidney stones?

11. What do all electromagnetic waves transfer?

12. What is the typical diameter of an atom (approximately)?

- [ ] **A** 0.02 nm
- [ ] **B** 0.2 nm
- [ ] **C** 2 nm
- [ ] **D** 20 nm

13. What do isotopes of an element have different numbers of?

- [ ] **A** electrons
- [ ] **B** neutrons
- [ ] **C** positrons
- [ ] **D** protons

14. What is represented by 59 in $^{59}_{27}$Co?

- [ ] **A** atomic number
- [ ] **B** mass number
- [ ] **C** neutron number
- [ ] **D** relative electric charge

15. What is the plum pudding model? 51

16. What happens during β^+ decay? 52

17. List the eight planets in increasing order of their distance from the Sun. 64

18. Which correctly describes the effects on the wavelength and frequency of an EM wave when red-shift occurs? 67

		Wavelength	Frequency
[ ]	**A**	decreases	decreases
[ ]	**B**	decreases	increases
[ ]	**C**	increases	decreases
[ ]	**D**	increases	increases

19. What happens to an object when a resultant force acts on it? 75

76 **20.** Which would have the biggest increase on the turning effect of a spanner?

- ☐ **A** A longer spanner with a smaller force.
- ☐ **B** A shorter spanner with a larger force.
- ☐ **C** A longer spanner with a larger force.
- ☐ **D** A shorter spanner with a smaller force.

76 **21.** What is the unit of the turning effect of a force?

....

79 **22.** Draw the electrical symbol for a diode.

81 **23.** What is the unit of electrical charge?

....

81 **24.** Define electric current.

....

....

84 **25.** What would you connect to a circuit to find the resistance of a component?

- ☐ **A** An ammeter and a voltmeter in parallel with the component.
- ☐ **B** An ammeter and a voltmeter in series with the component.
- ☐ **C** An ammeter in parallel and a voltmeter in series with the component.
- ☐ **D** An ammeter in series and a voltmeter in parallel with the component.

26. Which store is energy transferred to when an electric current flows in a resistor?

....

27. What formula is used to calculate electrical power?

- ☐ **A** $P = (IR)^2$
- ☐ **B** $P = I^2 \times R$
- ☐ **C** $P = I \times R$
- ☐ **D** $P = I \times R^2$

28. If a material loses electrons, what does it become?

- ☐ **A** negatively charged
- ☐ **B** neutral
- ☐ **C** positively charged
- ☐ **D** repellent to other electrons

29. On which type of materials can electric charge build up?

- ☐ **A** conductors
- ☐ **B** insulators
- ☐ **C** magnets
- ☐ **D** metals

30. What term is used to describe the removal of excess charge?

....

....

31. What is the name of the UK high voltage electric power transmission network?

....

32. Name the process by which a solid changes directly into a gas.

....

33. Which substances can be compressed?

- ☐ **A** gases only
- ☐ **B** solids and liquids
- ☐ **C** liquids only
- ☐ **D** solids only

34. What is 135.06 written to 2 significant figures?

- ☐ **A** 130
- ☐ **B** 135
- ☐ **C** 135.1
- ☐ **D** 140

35. Write 0.003 18 in standard form.

....

36. Convert 5000 W to MW.

- ☐ **A** 5×10^{-6} MW
- ☐ **B** 0.005 MW
- ☐ **C** 5 MW
- ☐ **D** 5 000 000 MW

37. Convert 76 A to mA.

- ☐ **A** 0.076 mA
- ☐ **B** 7.6 mA
- ☐ **C** 7600 mA
- ☐ **D** 76 000 mA

38. How can you convert μm to m?

- ☐ **A** divide by 1000
- ☐ **B** multiply by 1000
- ☐ **C** divide by 1 000 000
- ☐ **D** multiply by 1 000 000

2–6

Distance, speed and time

What's it all about?

Distance, speed and time are all physical quantities. Physical quantities are either scalar or vector.

	Scalar	Vector
Magnitude	Yes	Yes
Specific direction	No	Yes
Examples	• distance • speed • time • mass	• acceleration • momentum • velocity • displacement

Vector quantities can have both positive and negative values to show their direction.

Velocity is speed in a stated direction.

Displacement is distance in a stated direction.

Equations of motion

You need to be able to recall and apply these two equations.

Average speed

Objects often change speed during a journey, so it is better to use average speed:

average speed (m/s) = total distance travelled (m) ÷ total time taken (s)

Acceleration

Acceleration is a change in velocity per second. Acceleration is a vector quantity.

$$\text{acceleration (m/s}^2) = \frac{\text{change in velocity (m/s)}}{\text{time taken (s)}}$$

$$a = \frac{(v - u)}{t}$$

Velocity

Velocity is the change in distance per second.

Velocity is a vector quantity.

$$(\text{final velocity})^2 - (\text{initial velocity})^2 = 2 \times \text{acceleration} \times \text{distance}$$

$$v^2 - u^2 = 2 \times a \times x$$

Velocity/time graphs

Velocity/time graphs show how velocity changes with time. You can use them to find the acceleration of an object and the distance travelled.

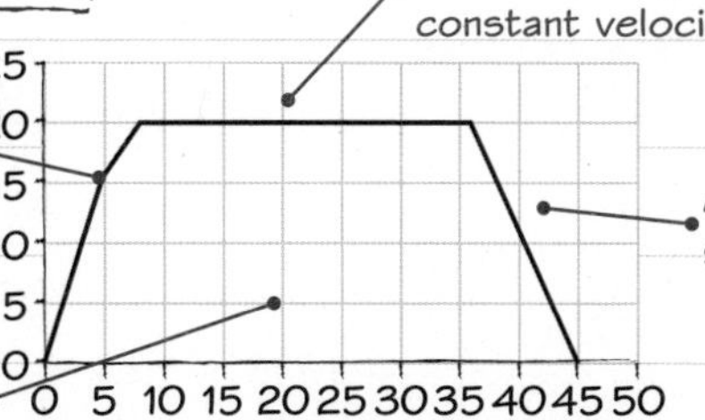

The gradient of the graph tells us the acceleration of the object. The steeper the slope, the higher the acceleration.

Velocity is plotted on the y-axis.

The area under the graph gives the distance travelled during that time.

A straight horizontal line means the object is travelling at a constant velocity.

A negative gradient shows deceleration.

Time is plotted on the x-axis.

Worked example

An athlete sprints from stationary with an acceleration of $8\,\text{m/s}^2$ for 5 m.

Calculate the velocity reached by the athlete. **(3 marks)**

$v^2 - u^2 = 2 \times a \times x$

$v^2 - 0^2 = 2 \times 8 \times 5$

$v^2 = 80$

$v = \sqrt{80} = 9\,\text{m/s}$ (rounded to 1 sf)

Substitute the given values into the correct equation. Simplify the equation and then calculate the answer.

The equation gives v^2 so you will need to find the square root.

Worked example

The diagram shows the velocity/time graph of a car.

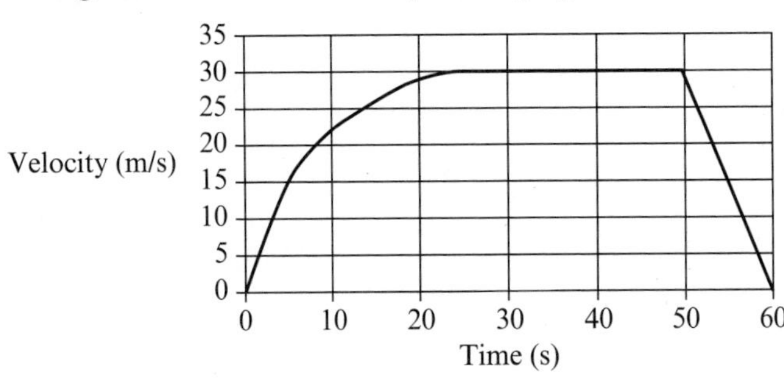

In the exam, you will only be asked to make velocity/time graph calculations relating to straight lines showing uniform acceleration or constant velocity.

(a) Calculate the acceleration of the car between 50 and 60 seconds. **(2 marks)**

acceleration = change in velocity ÷ time taken

$= \frac{0 - 30}{60 - 50}$

$= \frac{-30}{10}$

$= -3\,\text{m/s}^2$

Maths skills A negative gradient (downward slope) shows deceleration. Remember the – sign.

(b) Determine the distance travelled, in metres, m, between $t = 25$ seconds and when the car stops. **(3 marks)**

distance = area of rectangle + area of triangle

area of rectangle = $(50 - 25) \times 30 = 750\,\text{m}$

area of triangle = $0.5 \times (60 - 50) \times 30 = 150\,\text{m}$

distance travelled = $750 + 150 = 900\,\text{m}$

Maths skills Split the area into rectangles and triangles and find the areas of these shapes:

area of rectangle = length × width

area of triangle = $\frac{1}{2}$ × base × height

Exam practice

1. A cyclist increases speed from 5 m/s to 9 m/s with an acceleration of 1.2 m/s^2.

(a) Calculate the time taken for this acceleration to take place. **(3 marks)**

.... s

(b) Calculate the distance travelled during this acceleration. **(3 marks)**

.... m

Knowledge check

The equation you need is one you need to be able to recall.

Examiner's hint

Show each stage of the calculation as marks may be awarded for working even if your answer is wrong.

Use an equation from the formula sheet on page 73. This list will also be given to you with the exam paper.

Exam practice

2. The diagram shows a velocity/time graph for a train.

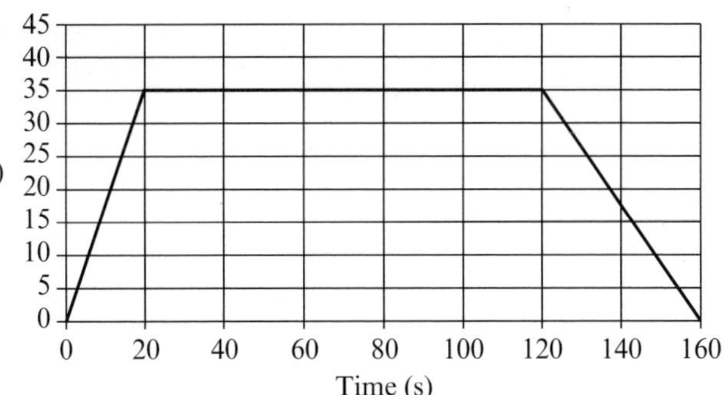

(a) Compare the distance travelled by the train when it is speeding up with the distance it travels at a constant velocity. **(4 marks)**

Clearly show the areas you are calculating from the graph.

You are told to compare the values after you have calculated them.

(b) Calculate the deceleration of the train between 120 and 160 seconds. **(3 marks)**

The train is slowing down so the acceleration must be negative.

Maths skills The values on the graph are given to 2 significant figures so give your answer in the same way.

.... m/s^2

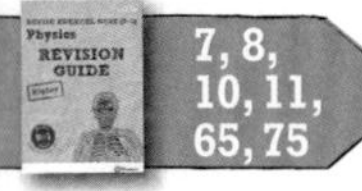
7, 8, 10, 11, 65, 75

Force, acceleration and circular motion

What's it all about?

Resultant force

If the forces acting on an object are balanced, the resultant force on the object is zero.

The object will stay still, or continue moving in a straight line at a constant speed and in the same direction.

You can calculate the resultant force acting on an object when you know its mass and acceleration, using Newton's second law.

force (N) = mass (kg) × acceleration (m/s^2)

$$F = m \times a$$

Circular motion

For circular motion to occur, there must be a force acting inwards along the radius of the circle. This is called the **centripetal force**. The object moves at **right angles** to this force.

One example of this is the motion of a satellite in orbit around the Earth.

If there were no forces acting on the satellite it would move in a straight line.

The gravitational force, acting towards the Earth, acts on the moving satellite. This is the **centripetal force** and it acts at 90° to the direction of motion of the satellite.

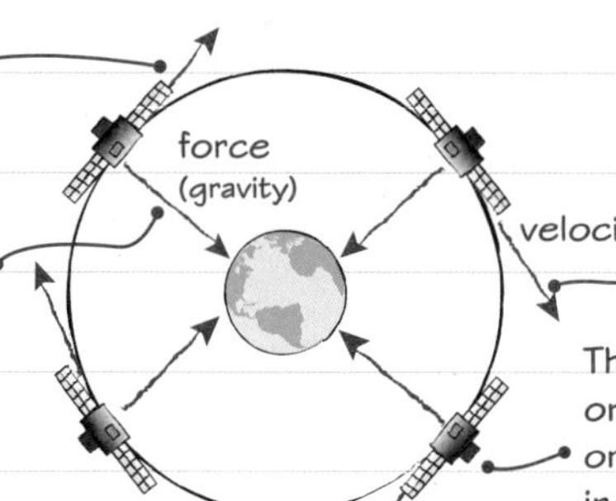

The speed of the satellite remains constant, but the velocity constantly changes due to the change in direction. This means that the satellite is accelerating even though it is travelling at a constant speed.

The speed of the satellite depends only on the mass of the planet and the orbital radius. If the orbital radius increases, the satellite slows down. If it decreases, the satellite speeds up.

Centripetal forces

 Gravitational, for example, an orbiting satellite.

 Frictional, for example, a car on a roundabout.

 Tension, for example, an Olympic hammer thrower.

Worked example

An object has no resultant force on it. Give two possible descriptions of its movement. **(2 marks)**

The object could be stationary or moving at a constant speed in a straight line.

Knowledge check

Remember to say the movement is in a straight line. If the direction is changing, the object has a changing velocity and is accelerating. Therefore the resultant force is not zero.

Worked example

The International Space Station (ISS) orbits the Earth.

(a) Explain what keeps the ISS in orbit. **(2 marks)**

An object accelerates if it has a resultant force acting on it. The force of gravity acts on the ISS giving it a resultant force towards the centre of the Earth (along the radius of its path). The ISS moves at right angles to this centripetal force, accelerating on a circular path.

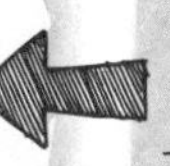

Synoptic link

This links with the topic about satellite orbits.

You are being asked to explain circular motion. Use correct physics terminology such as force, acceleration and centripetal.

(b) The mass of the ISS is 4.2×10^5 kg. The force acting on the ISS is 3700 kN.

Calculate the acceleration of the ISS in m/s^2. **(3 marks)**

$$F = m \times a$$

$$3700\,\text{kN} = 3\,700\,000\,\text{N} = 3.7 \times 10^6\,\text{N}$$

$$3.7 \times 10^6 = 4.2 \times 10^5 \times a$$

$$a = \frac{3.7 \times 10^6}{4.2 \times 10^5} = 8.8\,\text{m/s}^2$$

kg is the correct SI unit for mass, but kN needs to be converted to N.

The values given here are large numbers. Simplify your calculations as much as possible to avoid calculator errors.

Worked example

Define inertial mass. **(1 mark)**

It is the ratio of force over acceleration, $\frac{\text{force}}{\text{acceleration}}$. The larger an object, the more force is needed for it to accelerate.

Exam practice

1. This apparatus is used to investigate the effect of mass on acceleration.

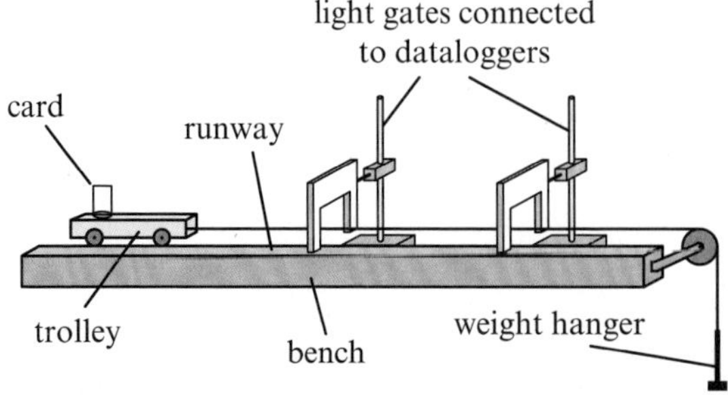

(a) Each light gate records the speed of the trolley as it passes through it. The time taken to travel between the light gates is also recorded.

Explain why two light gates are used. **(2 marks)**

(b) Give the reason why the number of masses on the hanger is kept constant. **(1 mark)**

(c) Give two reasons why the length of the string is important in this investigation. **(2 marks)**

(d) Give one safety precaution to take during this investigation. **(1 mark)**

Practical skills

If you are investigating the effect of **force** on acceleration, the overall mass of the moving items must remain the same. You move masses from the trolley to the hanger and take the measurements. This increases the pulling force on the trolley, but keeps the same accelerating mass.

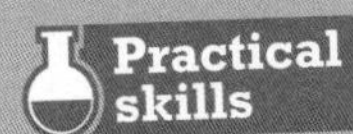

Consider what the string is used for in this investigation. What will happen if it is too long or too short?

Examiner's hint

You could be asked about different aspects of any of the core practicals.

Exam practice

2. A cyclist rides around a circular track.

(a) State what provides the centripetal force. **(1 mark)**

(b) Explain why the cyclist can travel at a constant speed, but not a constant velocity, around the track. **(2 marks)**

Think about the difference between speed and velocity. Your answer to an 'explain' question will normally need to include 'because', 'so', 'but' or 'therefore'.

3. A car and a lorry travel at the same speed. The same braking force is applied to both vehicles.

Explain why it takes more time for the lorry to stop than the car. **(3 marks)**

Consider the physics of the situation, including mass and acceleration.

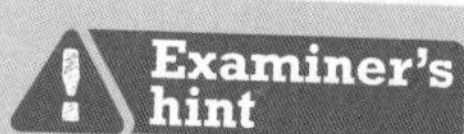

If you use the word 'longer', make sure it is clear whether you mean 'time' or 'distance'.

4. Calculate the acceleration of a 210 g ball with a resultant force of 3.4 N acting on it. **(3 marks)**

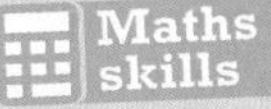

Remember to check the units.

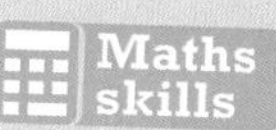

Give the answer to the same number of significant figures as the value in the question with the smallest number of significant figures.

12, 13

Momentum and collisions

What's it all about?

Momentum and force

Momentum is a **vector** quantity. It depends on an object's mass and velocity:

momentum (kg m/s) = mass (kg) × velocity (m/s)

$$p = m \times v$$

This is another way to write **Newton's second law**, usually shown as: $F = m \times a$

Force is the rate of change in momentum. It is also a vector quantity:

$$\text{force (N)} = \frac{\text{change in momentum (kg m/s)}}{\text{time take for change (s)}}$$

This can be rewritten as:

$$F = \frac{(mv - mu)}{t}$$

As the time taken, t, increases, the force, F, acting on an object decreases.

Collisions

Since momentum is a vector quantity, you must think about the direction of the moving object. Momentum has opposite signs (+ or −) for opposite directions.

Total momentum is the same after a collision as it is before the collision.

You can apply **Newton's third law** to collisions between objects:

- Colliding objects exert an equal and opposite force on each other.
- They are in contact for the same time (unless they then stick together).
- Momentum is conserved.

If objects stick together in a collision, you get one new object. Its mass is the total mass of the colliding objects.

The diagram shows two moving objects that collide, stick together and move off together.

If objects do not stick together in the collision, the number of objects and their masses stay the same. You calculate their individual momentums.

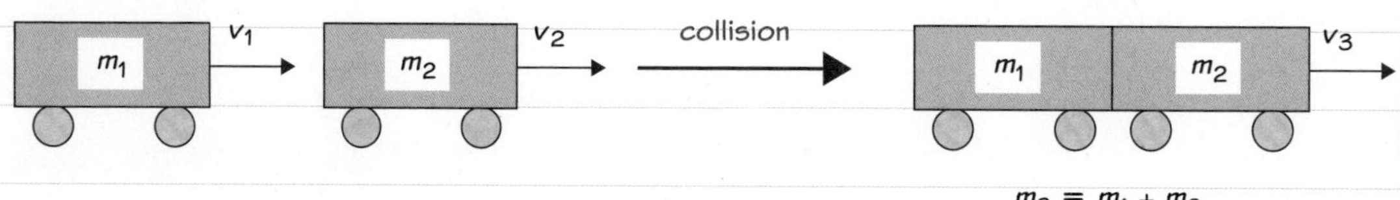

total momentum before the collision = total momentum after the collision

total mass after collision, $m_3 = m_1 + m_2$, so $(m_1 \times v_1) + (m_2 \times v_2) = m_3 \times v_3$

Worked example

(a) State Newton's third law when applied to a collision between two objects. **(1 mark)**

When two objects collide, they exert equal and opposite forces on each other.

(b) Explain how Newton's third law shows momentum is conserved when the two objects collide. **(3 marks)**

$$\text{force} = \frac{\text{change in momentum}}{\text{time for change}}$$

The force and time taken for the collision are the same for each object.

Therefore, the change in momentum for each object must also be the same but in opposite directions, so the overall change is zero.

Use the correct physics terms and be as concise as possible.

Worked example

An ice skater, mass 50 kg, skates at 5.0 m/s. The skater bumps into another skater, mass 45 kg, moving in the same direction at 2.0 m/s. They then slide together on the ice.

Calculate their velocity when they slide together.

(4 marks)

momentum before collision = momentum after collision

$p = m \times v$

momentum before = $(50 \times 5.0) + (45 \times 2.0)$

= 340 kg m/s

momentum after = $(50 + 45) \times v = 340$

$95 \times v = 340$

$$v = \frac{340}{95} = 3.6\text{ m/s}$$

Use the idea of conservation of momentum.

The total momentum before is the momentum of both skaters added together.

As the skaters are moving in the **same** direction, the momentum of both will be +.

As the skaters are now moving together, their masses need to be added together.

Give your answer to 2 sf as in the question.

Check your answer makes sense. After the collision, the faster skater will slow down and the slower skater will speed up, so the answer should be between 5 and 2 m/s.

Exam practice

1. A car travels at 25 m/s. The mass of the car and driver is 2500 kg. The driver applies the brakes for 0.5 s and the car slows down to 20 m/s.

   Calculate the force applied by the brakes. **(3 marks)**

   .... N

The equation linking force and change in momentum is given on the formula sheet in the exam paper. You will also find it on page 73.

2. A snooker player hits a white ball with a mass of 0.17 kg. It moves with an initial velocity of 0.82 m/s.

   (a) Calculate the initial momentum of the white ball. **(2 marks)**

   .... kg m/s

   (b) The white ball collides with a stationary red ball. After the collision, the white ball continues to move in the same direction with a velocity of 0.10 m/s. The red ball moves in the same direction with a velocity of 0.74 m/s.

   Calculate the mass of the red ball. **(3 marks)**

   .... kg

You need to be able to recall and use the equation for momentum.

Knowledge check

Collision questions will involve understanding, and use of, ideas about the conservation of momentum.

Exam practice

3. A car has a crumple zone. It is designed to bend and crush during a collision.

   Explain the effect of a crumple zone in a car on the force in a collision. **(3 marks)**

This links with knowledge about the hazards of large decelerations and how they can be reduced.

4. A cyclist travels at 6.0 m/s and takes 0.30 s to stop when hitting a post. The force acting on the bicycle is −1700 N.

   (a) Explain why the force has a negative sign. **(2 marks)**

   (b) Calculate the total mass of the cyclist and bicycle. **(3 marks)**

   .... kg

Check your answer by considering what would be a reasonable value for the mass of a person and a bicycle.

5. An electric toy train, with a mass of 0.30 kg, moves on a track with a velocity of 0.20 m/s. There is a stationary carriage on the track with a mass of 0.10 kg. The train hits the carriage and they move on together.

   Calculate the velocity of the train and carriage as they move on together. **(3 marks)**

   .... m/s

It is a good idea to draw a simple diagram showing the information you have.

For collisions where objects stick together, remember you may need to calculate the new mass.

13, 73, 74, 75

Force diagrams

What's it all about?

Free-body force diagrams

A free-body force diagram is a simplified diagram showing the forces acting on an object. The object is shown as a dot or a box. The force arrows act away from the dot or centre of the box. Balanced forces mean there is no resultant force. Unbalanced pairs show that there is acceleration.

A force is a vector quantity. It has direction as well as magnitude (size).

The longer the arrow, the larger the force. It is good practice to draw the arrows to scale.

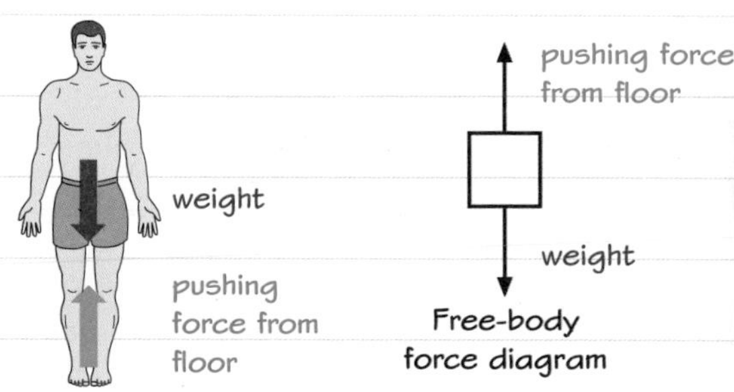

Vector diagrams and scale drawings

A resultant force can be resolved into its component horizontal and vertical forces by drawing a vector diagram.

A net force from two forces can also be found using scale drawings.

The horizontal and vertical components of motion do not affect one another – they are independent.

You can resolve a force into its horizontal and vertical components using a scale drawing on graph paper.

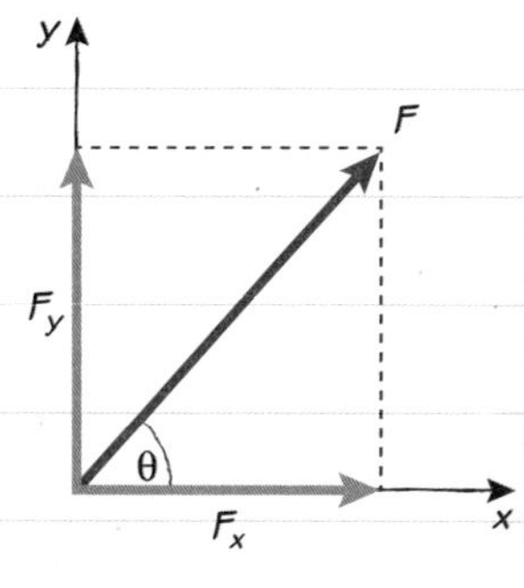

1. Decide on an appropriate scale. For example, for a force of 50 N acting at 60° to the horizontal, use a scale where 1 cm represents 10 N.
2. Using a ruler, protractor and pencil, draw a line at the correct angle to represent the force.

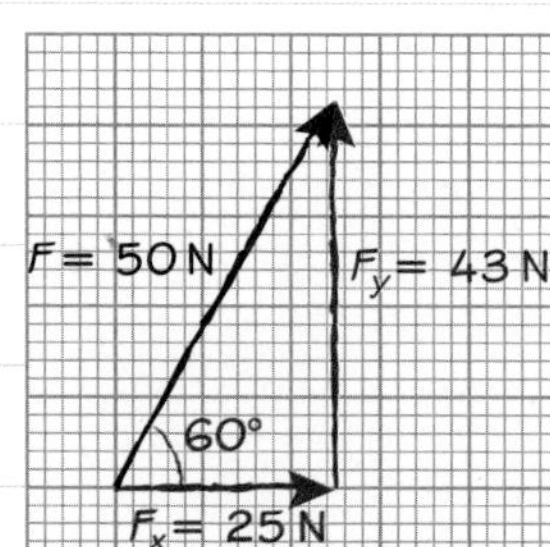

3. Draw the horizontal and vertical components.
4. Measure the lengths and convert to a force using the same scale.

Worked example

A ball has a weight of 5 N. Draw a free-body diagram of the ball accelerating on a floor with a forward force of 15 N. The friction force is 8 N. **(2 marks)**

normal contact 5 N

friction 8 N — forward 15 N

weight 5 N

Label each arrow with the force value and type. Different words are sometimes used to describe the same force e.g. forward, push, thrust.

Worked example

Draw a force of 600 N acting at 45° to the horizontal. Resolve the force into its horizontal and vertical components. Choose a suitable scale for the grid. **(3 marks)**

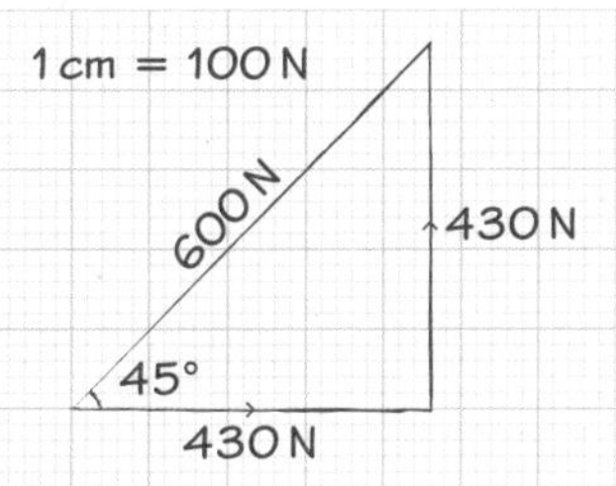

A suitable scale will usually mean the diagram fills at least half of the grid. In this case, 1 cm = 100 N is suitable.

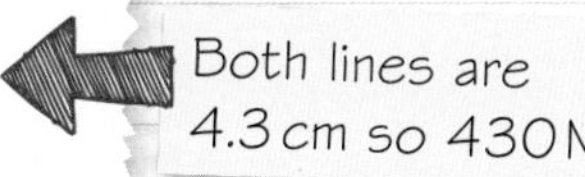

Worked example

A boat moves forwards with an engine force of 9000 N. A strong current of 2000 N pushes on the boat at an angle of 120° from the direction the boat is pointing.

Draw a scale diagram to work out the resultant force of these two forces on the boat. **(3 marks)**

2000 N

120° Resultant force on boat

60°

9000 N

Measure the resultant force arrow and convert from cm to N.

Choose a start point that will leave space to draw the force arrows. Then draw the information you are given to scale.

Draw a parallelogram; the diagonal is the resultant force.

Exam practice

1. Draw a labelled free-body diagram of the balanced forces on a cup on a shelf. The cup weighs 2.5 N. **(1 mark)**

2. A drone moves upwards with a resultant vertical force of 20 N. A resultant horizontal wind force of 8 N to the right acts on the drone.

   (a) Draw a free-body force diagram for the drone. **(2 marks)**

   (b) Draw a scale drawing to show the overall resultant force on the drone. Include the value of the force. **(2 marks)**

3. A child holds a flying kite at an angle of 65° to the horizontal. The tension in the string is 30 N.

   Draw a scale drawing to find the vertical and horizontal components of this force. **(3 marks)**

Synoptic link

Action–reaction (a–r) forces are not the same as balanced forces. In both cases, the forces are equal and act in opposite directions, but a–r forces act on different objects while balanced forces all act on the same object.

Remember to label the force arrows and indicate their sizes.

Maths skills

Scale drawings must be drawn very accurately.

Maths skills

You may need to measure angles. You will be told whether to measure the angle against the horizontal or the vertical.

Maths skills

For a scale drawing of forces involving a right angle, you can use Pythagoras' theorem to check the answers ($a^2 + b^2 = c^2$).

Exam practice

4. A child is sitting still halfway down a sloping slide.

   (a) Give an example of force pairs that obey Newton's third law in this situation. **(1 mark)**

   (b) Draw a free-body force diagram of the child sitting still on the slide. **(1 mark)**

Synoptic link

Newton's third law states that whenever two objects interact, they exert equal and opposite forces on each other. It is about forces on two *different* objects when they interact, either through contact or at a distance. Non-contact forces include magnetism, static electricity and gravitational force. When objects touch, there are contact forces, such as friction, normal contact force, upthrust, tension and air resistance.

5. A cannon ball is fired with a firing force of 70 N at an angle of 40° from the horizontal.

   Draw a scale drawing to resolve the horizontal and vertical components of the firing force. **(3 marks)**

76, 77

Rotational forces

What's it all about?

Moments

Forces which act at a **distance** from a **pivot** can cause a **turning effect** or rotation. This is known as a **moment**.

You can calculate a moment using the equation:

moment (newton-metres, Nm) = force (N) × distance normal to the direction of the force (m)

The size of the turning force depends on the magnitude of the applied force, and the distance of the applied force from the pivot.

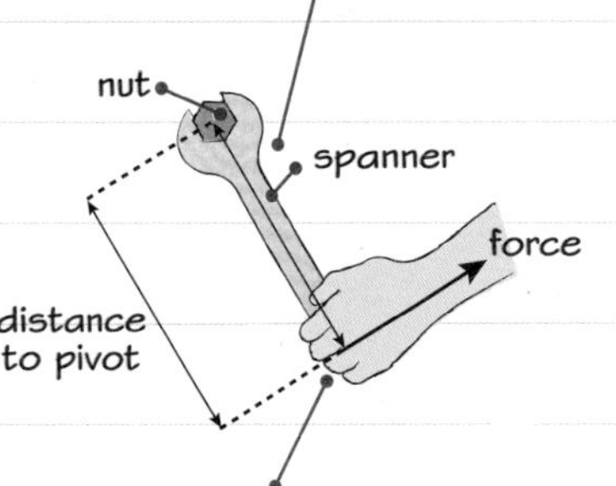

The force applied to the spanner produces a turning force at the pivot which turns the nut.

Levers

Levers transmit the rotational effects of forces.

As a cyclist applies an input force to the brake lever, the lever turns on the pivot.

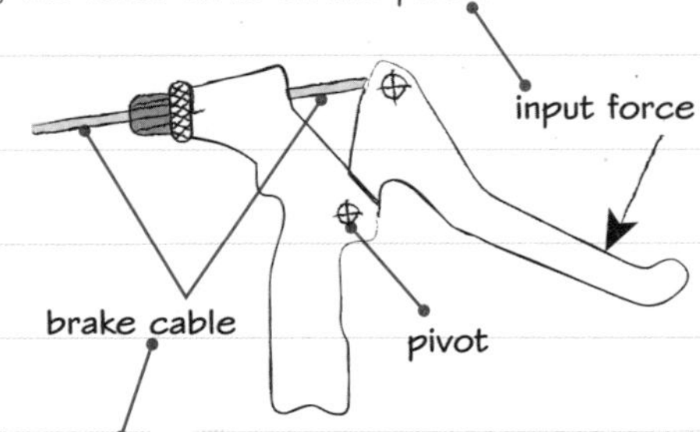

An output force is produced which pulls on the brake cable and causes the brake pads to press against the wheel. The size of the output force depends on the size of the input force applied to the brake lever.

When rotational forces are in equilibrium: the sum of the clockwise moments = the sum of the anti-clockwise moments

Gears

Gears are toothed wheels that join together to transmit rotational forces and motion.

A low gear is when a smaller input gear turns a larger output gear. This leads to a **low speed** and a **high turning effect**.

A high gear is when a large input gear turns a smaller output gear. This leads to a **high speed** and a **low turning effect**.

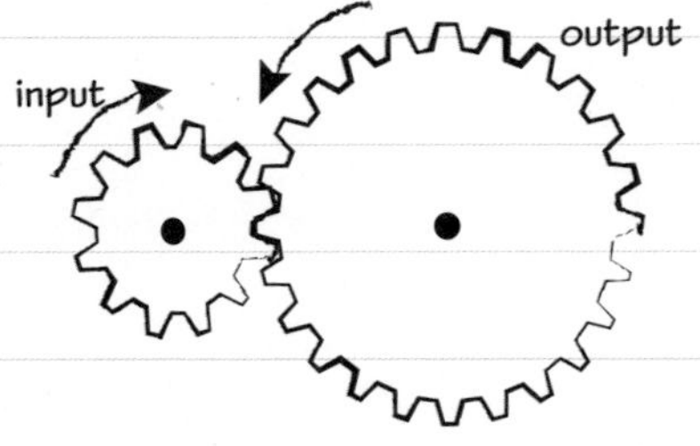

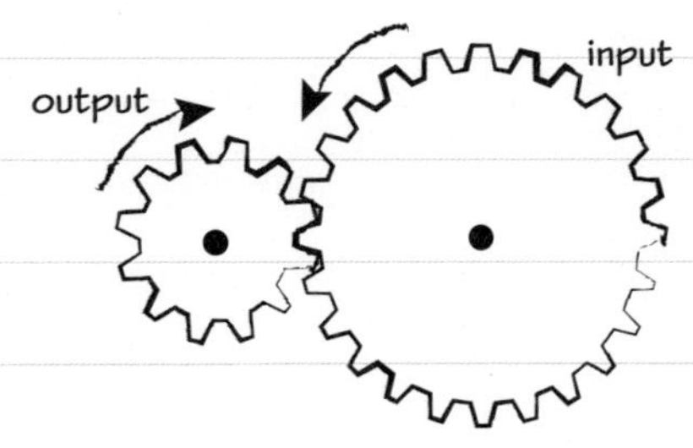

Worked example

The diagram shows a crowbar being used as a lever. A force is applied to the crowbar to lift up a drain cover.

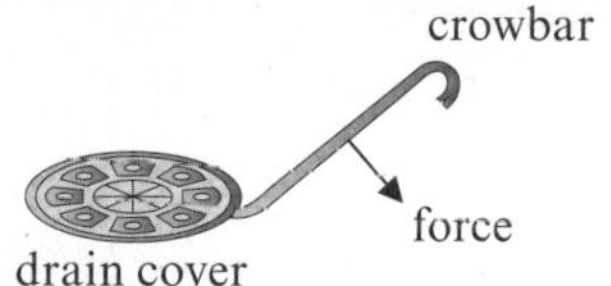

(a) Describe how the force needed to lift the cover will change with the position at which the force is applied to the crowbar. **(2 marks)**

The pivot is where the crowbar meets the ground. The further from the pivot the force is applied, the less force will be needed to produce the same turning effect to lift up the cover.

(b) A force of 60 N is applied at a perpendicular distance of 0.60 m from the pivot.

Calculate the moment of the force. **(2 marks)**

moment of force = force × perpendicular distance
= 60 × 0.60
= 36 Nm

'Distance normal to the direction of the force' is often written as 'perpendicular distance'. They both mean 'the distance at right angles to the force'. This is also the shortest distance between the pivot and the line of action of the force.

Worked example

The diagram shows a wooden beam with a weight of 120 N and a length of 1 m. It rests on a pivot. A rope is used to hold up one end of the beam so it is balanced.

tension force in rope
weight
pivot
0.1 m

Calculate the tension force in the rope. **(3 marks)**

clockwise moment = anticlockwise moment
moment = force × perpendicular distance
anticlockwise moment = 120 × 0.1 = 12 Nm
clockwise moment = tension × 0.6 m = 12 Nm
tension force = $\frac{12}{0.6}$ = 20 N

The downwards force is the weight of the beam acting at the centre of the beam (0.5 m from either end).

First work out the moment for which you have both force and distance values.

The distance from the tension force to the pivot is half the length of the beam (where the weight acts) plus 0.1 m. Distance = 0.5 + 0.1 = 0.6 m

Exam practice

1. Anuj, who weighs 350 N, sits on the right-hand side of a seesaw 1.5 m from the pivot. Khalil, who weighs 300 N, sits on the other side of the pivot.

   Calculate the distance from the pivot Khalil must sit to balance the seesaw. **(3 marks)**

   distance from pivot = ... m

Examiner's hint

Moments calculations only involve one equation and one principle so make sure you learn them.

2. The diagram shows a hanging mobile. The mobile is balanced.

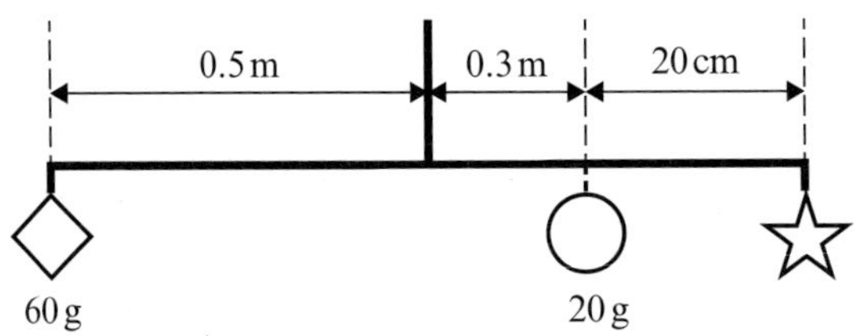

(a) Describe the conditions needed for the mobile to be balanced. **(1 mark)**

There are two forces causing clockwise moments so make sure you find the total.

(b) Calculate the mass of the star. **(4 marks)**

mass = ... g

Maths skills

In this example, $F = W = mg$. As both sides of the equation are multiplied by the gravitational field strength, g, it can be ignored. Also, there is no need to convert g to kg in this example.

Exam practice

3. A gear wheel with 30 teeth turns once clockwise. It turns a smaller gear wheel with 6 teeth.

   Describe the motion of the smaller gear wheel during one turn of the larger gear wheel. **(1 mark)**

Think about both the direction of movement of the smaller gear and the number of turns it will make.

4. The diagram shows a wheelbarrow being lifted.

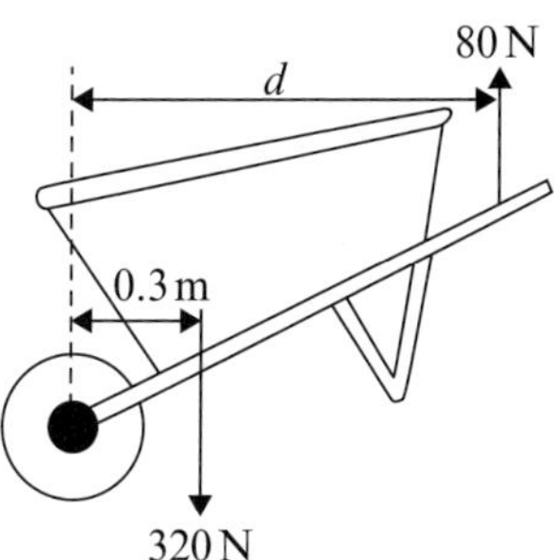

The weight of the wheelbarrow is 320 N. It acts at a perpendicular distance of 0.3 m from the pivot.

Calculate the distance, d, at which a force of 80 N can be applied to lift and balance the wheelbarrow. **(3 marks)**

This is similar to the second worked example.

.... m

5. The diagram shows a girl fishing with a 1.5 m long rod. She catches a fish which pulls with a force of 24 N. She pulls back on the rod 0.3 m from the pivot.

   Calculate the force needed to pull the fish out of the water.

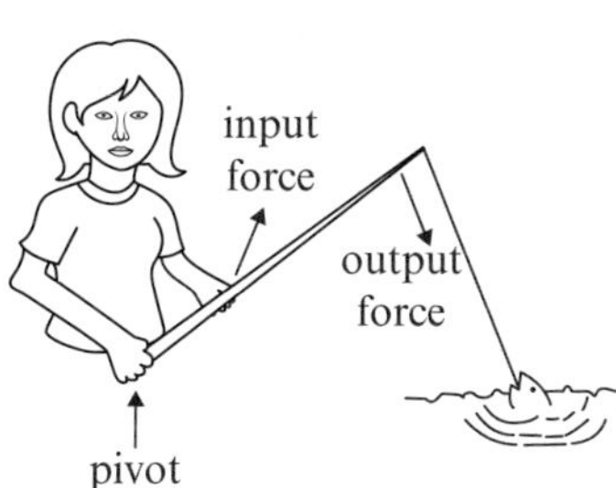

(3 marks)

Calculate the force needed for the equilibrium situation.

To pull the fish out of the water, the anticlockwise moment needs to be greater than the clockwise moment. A force **larger** than the equilibrium force is needed.

.... N

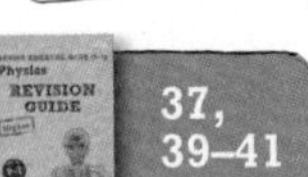

37, 39–41

Radiation and temperature

What's it all about?

Electromagnetic radiation

All objects with a temperature above absolute zero emit electromagnetic radiation. The intensity and the wavelength of the emission depend on the temperature of the object.

When a body is at a constant temperature, it radiates and absorbs radiation at the same average power. If they are not equal the object will either heat up or cool down.

Absolute zero is the temperature at which particles have no kinetic energy or movement. The scale is kelvin (K) and absolute zero is 0 K or −273 °C. To convert from kelvin to Celsius, subtract 273 from the temperature in kelvin.

Electromagnetic spectrum

The different types of electromagnetic radiation are shown in the electromagnetic spectrum.

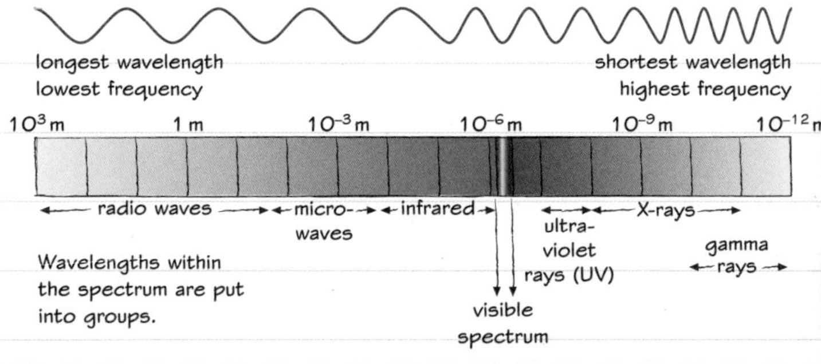

Intensity and wavelength

Intensity is the energy emitted per m^2 per second. As an object gets hotter, intensity increases and more energy is transferred by radiation. As the temperature rises, the wavelength of the radiation emitted at maximum or peak intensity decreases, so the radiation moves towards the higher energy end of the spectrum.

Hot objects emit radiation at the red end of the visible light spectrum and some glow red. As radiation moves towards the blue end of the visible light spectrum, the object becomes red-orange, then white hot.

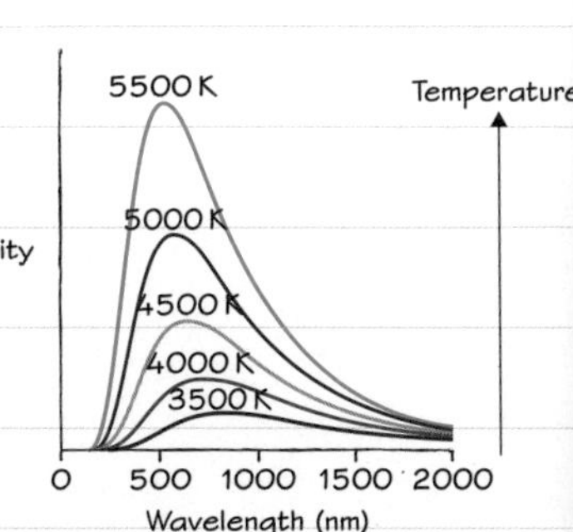

Worked example

Explain the factors that affect the temperature of the Earth in terms of the balance between radiation absorbed and emitted. **(6 marks)**

The Earth's temperature depends on the rates at which radiation is absorbed and emitted by the Earth's surface and atmosphere. If the rates are equal, the temperature will remain constant.

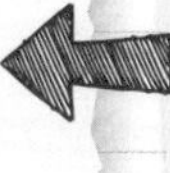

Use physics to explain what causes temperature changes on Earth in terms of the balance between absorption and emission of radiation.

Absorption: Visible light and high-frequency infrared radiation are absorbed by the surface of the Earth, causing it to get hotter.

Describe the processes that heat the Earth.

Emission: The Earth radiates lower-frequency infrared radiation through the atmosphere into space. Energy is also transferred to the atmosphere by conduction and convection from the Earth's surface. These processes cause the Earth to cool.

Describe the processes that cool the Earth.

Worked example

Explain why average global temperatures are increasing. **(4 marks)**

Greenhouse gases in the atmosphere absorb infrared radiation emitted from the Earth. The greenhouse gases also emit infrared radiation in all directions. Some is sent into space and some is reabsorbed by the Earth's surface. The concentration of greenhouse gases in the atmosphere is increasing. This causes more infrared radiation to be reabsorbed by the Earth. This increase in absorption means the rate of absorption is now higher than the rate of emission, hence average global temperatures are increasing.

Explain the effect of the concentration of greenhouse gases on the Earth's temperature.

Exam practice

1. (a) Describe the relationship between the temperature of a body and the wavelength of the radiation it emits. **(1 mark)**

(b) State the type of radiation emitted by a hot kettle. **(1 mark)**

(c) The graph shows the intensity of radiation for different wavelengths emitted from a warm object.

Draw a line on the graph showing the radiation emitted from the same object at a much higher temperature. **(2 marks)**

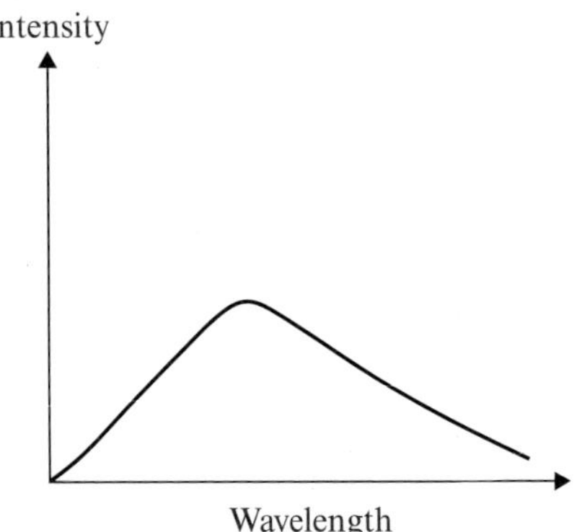

What is the relationship between intensity, wavelength and temperature?

Remember, the lines should not cross.

2. Explain why the temperature of an electric heater rises and then remains at a constant value. **(3 marks)**

$$\text{power (W)} = \frac{\text{energy change (J)}}{\text{time taken}}$$

Exam practice

3. Hot water is put into a sealed, shiny, white metal container. The temperature just outside the container is measured at regular intervals. The graph shows how the temperature changes over time.

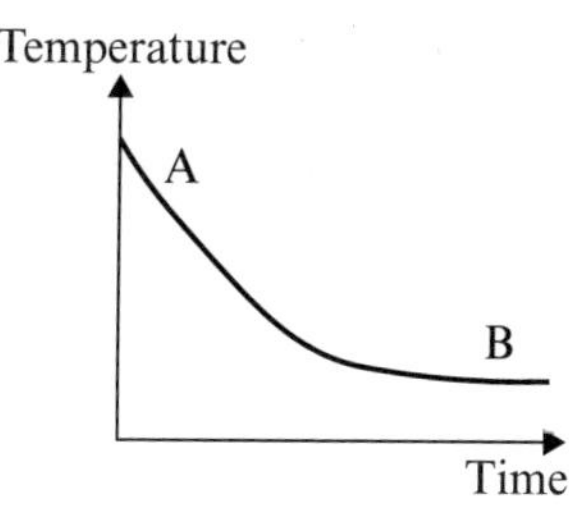

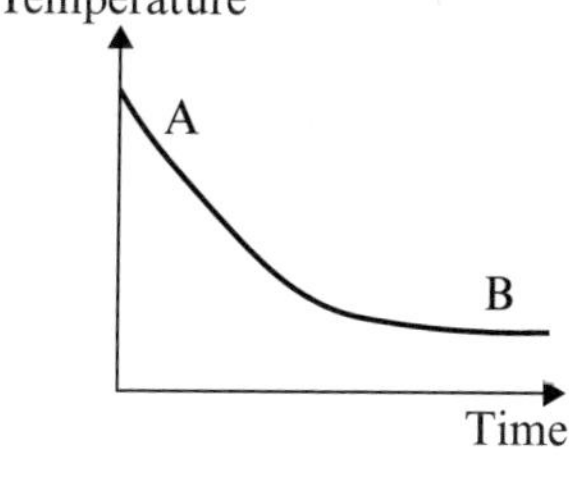

(a) Explain what is happening to the container at:

(i) point A on the graph. **(2 marks)**

(ii) point B on the graph. **(1 mark)**

(b) Sketch a line on the graph to show the result you would expect if an identical experiment was carried out using a black, matt container. **(2 marks)**

4. (a) An infrared camera produces an image of an animal. The image shows up as different colours.

Explain why. **(2 marks)**

(b) The infrared camera can detect radiation with a wavelength of 12 μm. The velocity of electromagnetic waves is 3×10^8 m/s.

Calculate the frequency of this radiation. Give your answer in standard form. **(4 marks)**

.... Hz

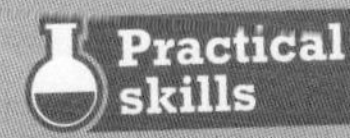

This question relates to one of your core practicals.

Knowledge check

Black, matt bodies radiate and absorb thermal energy at a higher rate than light, shiny ones.

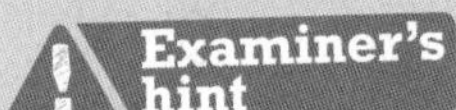

'Explain' means you need to say what is happening and also give a reason why.

$v = f \times \lambda$

Maths skills

1 μm = 0.000 001 m. To convert μm to m, divide by 1 000 000.

26–29

Speed and uses of sound

What's it all about?

If a sound wave moves from one material to another, the frequency stays the same.

If the wave speed increases or decreases, the wavelength does the same.

wave speed (m/s) = frequency (Hz) × wavelength (m)

$$v = f \times \lambda$$

Refraction and reflection of sound waves at boundaries

The diagram shows a wave front slowing down as it moves from one material into another. The wave refracts because the densities of the materials are different.

Sound waves can refract and change speed and wavelength when moving from one material to another.

If they hit the boundary at an angle other than 90° they will also change direction.

Sound waves travel in medium 1 at an angle size i to the normal.

medium 1

They refract in medium 2 and travel at an angle size r to the normal.

medium 2

boundary

The wavelength, and hence the wave speed, both decrease.

Ultrasound

Sound waves can also reflect when they hit boundaries with a different density. This has many uses, particularly with ultrasound.

For calculations involving wave speed, distance and time, use:

$$\text{wave speed (m/s)} = \frac{\text{distance (m)}}{\text{time (s)}}$$

$$v = \frac{x}{t}$$

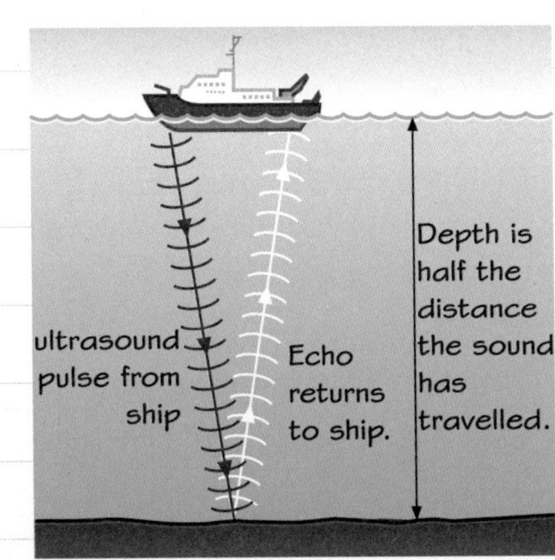

The human ear can only detect sounds between 20 Hz and 20 000 Hz. Low-pitched sounds below 20 Hz are called infrasound. High-pitched sounds above 20 000 Hz are called ultrasound.

Worked example

Seismic waves are infrasound waves. Explain how seismic waves can be used to study the Earth's core. **(3 marks)**

The layers in the Earth have different densities. The infrasound waves are refracted at the layer boundaries. S-waves only travel through solids. P-waves travel through solids and liquids. This allows scientists to interpret information about the core and the materials it is made from.

Worked example

Explain how ultrasound is used to create an image of a foetus. **(4 marks)**

When ultrasound waves are directed at the foetus, some of the waves are reflected at the boundaries between different tissues.

The time taken for the waves to leave the source and return to the detector is recorded. This is then used to calculate the distances between the tissues, so an image of the foetus can be created.

Ultrasound waves are harmless to the unborn baby.

Worked example

Engineers detect a fault inside the foundation stone of a building. Ultrasound waves travel from a source to the fault and back to the detector in 3.5 ms. The speed of sound in the stone is 3900 m/s.

Calculate how far inside the stone the fault is. **(4 marks)**

$v = \frac{x}{t}$

Convert 3.5 ms to 0.0035 s

$3900 = \frac{x}{0.0035}$

$x = 3900 \times 0.0035 = 13.65\text{ m}$

$\frac{13.65}{2} = 6.825\text{ m}$

Distance to the fault inside the stone = 6.8 m

0.0035 s is the time it takes to get from the source to the fault and back again.

The distance to the fault is half this distance.

Give your answer to 2 sf, the same as the given values.

Exam practice

1. (a) Which of these is an ultrasound wave? **Tick** one box. **(1 mark)**

☐ 21 Hz ☐ 210 Hz ☐ 2.1 kHz ☐ 21 kHz

(b) Explain how ultrasound waves, transmitted into the water from a boat, are used to detect shoals of fish. **(3 marks)**

(c) The boat detects echoes from a shoal of fish after 20 ms. The speed of sound in water is 1500 m/s.

Calculate the distance of the shoal from the boat. **(4 marks)**

.... m

(d) Explain why ultrasound waves can be used to remove dirt from a bike chain in a liquid. **(2 marks)**

Check the units.

Maths skills

To convert ms to s, divide by 1000.

Examiner's hint

A common error with sonar and other echo calculations is using the incorrect distance. Remember, the sound travels to the object and back again.

Knowledge check

Sound waves transfer energy. Vibrations cause particles to move as the wave passes through different materials.

Exam practice

2. Sound waves move faster in warm air than cold air.

(a) Complete the wave front diagram to show what happens as sound waves move from warm air to cold air. **(2 marks)**

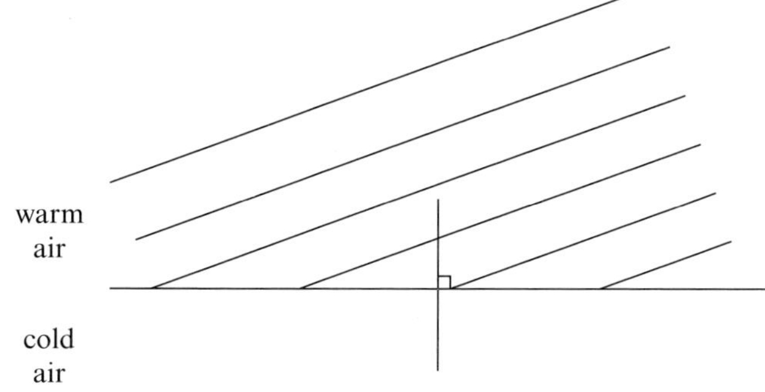

Showing what happens at wave fronts during refraction applies to all waves.

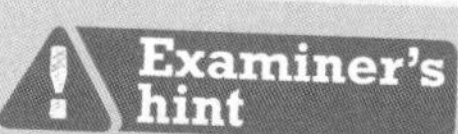

Use a sharp pencil and ruler to draw your answer accurately.

Knowledge check

When the speed decreases, the wavelength decreases.

(b) Describe the effect on the waves of a further increase in temperature at the air boundary. **(2 marks)**

Think about the effect of the change in temperature on the wave and how this will affect what happens at the boundary.

(c) In the warm air, a sound wave has a wavelength of 0.040 m and a speed of 340 m/s. The wavelength in cold air is 0.035 m.

Calculate the speed of the same sound wave in the cold air. **(3 marks)**

Examiner's hint

Check your answer makes sense.
The speed in cold air should be less than the speed in warm air.

.... m/s

21, 71

Energy, power and efficiency

What's it all about?

Gravitational potential energy

Gravitational potential energy is the energy an object has due to its height above the ground. It also depends on the mass of the object and the gravitational field strength, which is usually given as $g = 10$ N/kg.

The change in gravitational potential energy is given by the equation:

change in gravitational potential energy (J) = mass (kg) × gravitational field strength (N/kg) × change in vertical height (m)

$$\Delta GPE = m \times g \times \Delta h$$

Kinetic energy

A moving object has kinetic energy which depends on its mass and speed.

Kinetic energy is stored in moving objects and is calculated using the eqution:

Kinetic energy (J) = $\frac{1}{2}$ × mass (kg) × $(\text{speed})^2$ $(\text{m/s})^2$

$$KE = \frac{1}{2} \times m \times v^2$$

Energy transfers

Energy can be transferred and stored differently within a system. If the system is closed, the total energy remains the same. The rate at which **energy is transferred** (or the rate of **work done**) is the **power**.

$$\text{power (W)} = \frac{\text{energy transferred (J)}}{\text{time taken (s)}}$$

Power is measured in watts. 1 watt is 1 joule of energy transferred every second. Energy transferred also equals the **work done**.

work done (J) = force (N) × distance travelled in the direction of the force (m)

Efficiency

Energy transfers can be useful or wasted. The efficiency of energy transfers can be found using the following equation.

efficiency =

$$\frac{\text{useful energy transferred by the device}}{\text{total energy supplied to the device}}$$

Efficiency has a value between 0 and 1 and can also be given as a percentage (%).

Worked example

Water is pumped from a lake up to a storage reservoir.

You could also work this out using the equation: work done = force × distance moved.

(a) 5 kg of water gains 11 000 J in its gravitational potential energy store when it is pumped from the lake up to the reservoir.

Calculate the height of the reservoir above the lake. (gravitational field strength (g) = 10 N/kg) **(3 marks)**

$11000 = 5 \times 10 \times \Delta h$

$11000 = 50 \times \Delta h$

$\Delta h = \frac{11000}{50} = 220\,\text{m}$

Multiplying 5 by 10 to get 50 gives you one less number to work with.

All the equations used on this page are ones you need to learn.

(b) 5 kg of water is released back down into the lake.

Calculate the speed of the water as it hits the lake. **(3 marks)**

$11000 = \frac{1}{2} \times 5 \times v^2$

$11000 = 2.5 \times v^2$

$v^2 = \frac{11000}{2.5} = 4440$

$v = \sqrt{4400} = 66\,\text{m/s}$

The water falls the same height as it was raised. Assume that all the GPE is transferred into KE, so KE = 11000 J.

Remember to square root v^2 to find v.

(c) The falling water flows through a turbine that transfers 7.9×10^4 MJ in 60 seconds.

Calculate the power of the turbine. **(3 marks)**

energy transferred $= 7.9 \times 10^4\,\text{MJ} = 7.9 \times 10^{10}\,\text{J}$

$\text{power} = \frac{7.9 \times 10^{10}}{60}$

$= 1.3 \times 10^9\,\text{W}$

Convert MJ to J: 1 MJ = 10^6 J.

(d) The turbine has an efficiency of 0.4.

Calculate how much useful energy is transferred by the turbine in 60 seconds. **(2 marks)**

$0.4 = \frac{\text{useful energy transferred by the device}}{7.9 \times 10^4\,\text{MJ}}$

useful energy transferred by the device = $0.4 \times 7.9 \times 10^4\,\text{MJ} = 3.2 \times 10^4\,\text{MJ}$

Because efficiency is a ratio, any unit can be used for useful and total energy, as long as the same units are chosen.

Exam practice

A motor pulls a car up a rollercoaster slope with a vertical height of 30 m. The car gains 240 kJ of gravitational potential energy.

(a) Calculate the mass of the car.

(gravitational field strength (g) = 10 N/kg) **(3 marks)**

mass = ... kg

(b) The motor takes 25 seconds to pull the car to the top of the slope.

(i) Calculate the power of the motor. Give the correct unit. **(3 marks)**

power = ... unit ....

(ii) Explain why the actual power of the motor is likely to be higher than the power you have calculated. **(2 marks)**

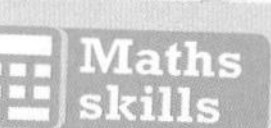

You need to remember the equations for kinetic energy and gravitational potential energy.

Remember to convert any units into the ones needed for each equation.

Remember to write down the unit for power – there is 1 mark for it.

Examiner's hint

Answers to 'explain' questions need reasons.

Exam practice

(c) The car drops 20 m from the top of the slope.

Calculate the speed of the car 20 m below the top of the slope. **(3 marks)**

Knowledge check As the car drops, GPE is transferred to KE. The sum of the GPE and KE is always the same.

Maths skills The best way to do this is to combine the equations for GPE and KE.

speed = ... m/s

(d) The emergency brakes are applied and the car comes to a stop in 40 m. The work done by the brakes is 270 000 J.

Calculate the force applied by the brakes. **(2 marks)**

Knowledge check Use one of the equations you have learned.

force = ... N

48–50, 55–57

Ionising radiation

What's it all about?

Properties of radiation

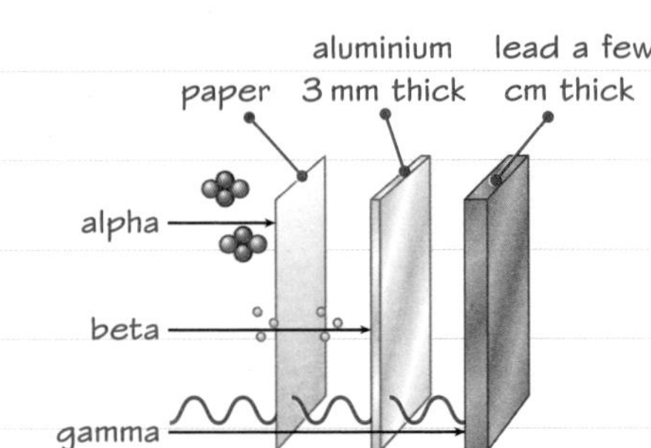

Alpha and beta particles and gamma-rays can collide with atoms, ionising them by causing them to lose electrons. Neutrons:

- are not directly ionising
- have a very high penetrating power due to them having no charge and not interacting strongly with matter.

Alpha particles are very ionising and travel up to 5 cm in air.

Beta particles are moderately ionising and travel up to 2 m in air.

Gamma rays are weakly ionising and travel hundreds of metres in air.

Background radiation

Low levels of radiation are around us all the time. This is known as **background radiation** and can be natural or generated by human activities.

Natural		Generated by human activities	
Radon gas	Produced when uranium in rocks decays – diffuses in soil and rocks and can build up in homes	Nuclear power stations	Leakage
Food and drink	Absorbed through roots from soil	Hospitals	Radioactive materials used and made
Cosmic rays	Charged particles from Sun and other stars		

Detecting and measuring radioactivity

Photographic film and a Geiger–Müller tube can both be used to measure and detect radiation. A Geiger–Müller (GM) tube is connected to a counter or ratemeter which shows the amount of radiation that has been detected.

Exposure

Irradiation: exposure from outside the body to harmful rays, e.g. gamma rays and beta particles

Exposure to radioactive materials

Contamination

Internal: eaten, drunk or breathed in

External: contact with hair, skin and clothing

Worked example

A scientist measures the activity of a radioisotope using a GM tube and a ratemeter. The radioisotope is stored in a lead box when not in use.

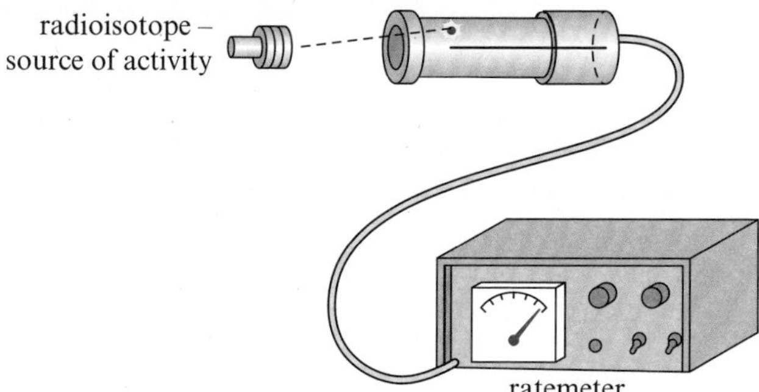

(a) The scientist handles the radioisotope with tongs.

Explain how using tongs minimises the risk of irradiation and contamination for the scientist. **(2 marks)**

The scientist uses tongs to hold the radioisotope away from their body. This reduces the effects of irradiation as intensity decreases with distance. It also prevents contamination as the scientist has no direct contact with the radioisotope.

Use key terms to show your understanding when giving explanations.

The 'true activity' does not include background radiation.

(b) Describe a method to measure the true activity of the radioisotope. **(4 marks)**

You are asked to describe a method, so write it in a logical way.

Place the radioisotope in front of the GM tube.

Record the count rate every 30 seconds for 2 minutes. Remove the radioisotope away from the GM tube and put it back in the lead box. Record the count rate every 30 seconds for 2 minutes. This is the background count.

Choose to take enough readings to obtain an average.

If the source is in a lead box, it should not affect the background count.

Calculate the average count rates for both the radioisotope, and the background. Subtract the background count rate from the count rate for the radioisotope. This is the true activity of the source.

Remember to say what you need to do with the measurements to find the true activity.

Exam practice

1. Compare the penetration of alpha, beta and gamma radiation through air, paper and aluminium. **(3 marks)**

Examiner's hint

A 'compare' question requires you to look for similarities **or** differences between things.

Your answer should mention all three types of radiation.

2. Compare the hazards of radioactive contamination and irradiation. **(6 marks)**

Your answer should mention the hazards of both contamination and irradiation.

State clearly what contamination and irradiation are, then consider the hazards of each.

For 6-mark questions, plan and write your answers in a logical way. Use relevant scientific terms.

A conclusion is not needed for a 'compare' question.

Exam practice

3. A manufacturer is considering the best radioisotope to use as the source in their smoke detectors.

The possible radioisotopes are given in the table.

Radioisotope	Radiation emitted	Half-life
Americium-241	alpha	432 years
Cobalt-60	gamma	5.27 years
Neptunium-235	alpha	396 days
Nickel-53	beta	100 years

Evaluate which radioisotope the company should use.

Your answer should describe the properties of all the radioisotopes. **(6 marks)**

Examiner's hint

An 'evaluate' question requires you to review information, such as data in a table – for instance, by considering advantages and disadvantages of different situations. Then you need to reach a conclusion which relates back to the question.
In this case, choose the best isotope from the list for a smoke detector, and support your choice with scientific reasoning.

You can continue your answer on a separate piece of paper.

4. (a) Explain what is meant by background radiation.
(2 marks)

(b) Give **two** sources of background radiation.
(2 marks)

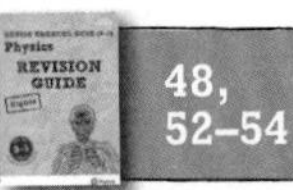
48, 52–54

Radioactive decay

What's it all about?

Nuclear decay

Atoms of a radioactive substance have unstable nuclei which decay and emit radiation in a random process. Each type of radioactive decay has a different effect on the nucleus.

Type of radiation emitted	Particle symbol	Change in the nucleus	
		Mass	Charge
alpha, α	$^{4}_{2}He$ or $^{4}_{2}\alpha$	−4	−2
beta minus, β− (electron)	$^{0}_{-1}e$ or $^{0}_{-1}\beta$	0	+1
beta plus β+ (positron)	$^{0}_{+1}e$ or $^{0}_{+1}\beta$	0	−1
neutron, n	$^{1}_{0}n$	−1	0
gamma, γ	EM radiation	0	0

In any nuclear decay, the total:
- mass is conserved
- charge is conserved.

To write or balance a nuclear equation

Ignore the mass of the β-particle as it is so small and written as 0.

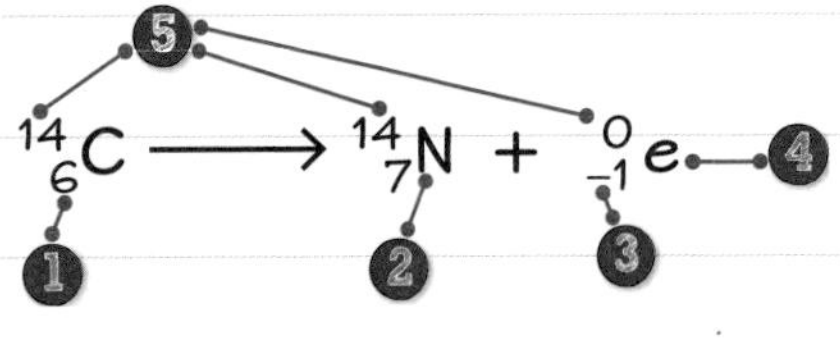

1. Look at the nucleus that is decaying: what are its mass and charge?
2. Look at the daughter nucleus: what are its mass and charge?
3. Look at the type of decay: what are its mass and charge?
4. Write the equation; work out any missing masses and charges.
5. Check that total mass and total charge are the same before and after the decay.

Half life

The half-life of a radioactive isotope is the **time** taken for half of the undecayed nuclei to decay. It is also the time taken for the **activity** of a source to decrease by half. Activity is the number of nuclear decays per second, measured in Becquerels (Bq).

For example, a radioactive isotope has a half-life of 2 hours.

If the initial activity is 100 Bq, after 2 hours it will be 50 Bq, after 4 hours it will be 25 Bq, after 6 hours it will be 12.5 Bq, and so on.

Worked example

Balance the nuclear equation for this decay. Radon-220 undergoes α decay to form an isotope of polonium. **(2 marks)**

$^{220}_{86}\text{Ra} \rightarrow {}^{216}_{84}\text{Po} + {}^{4}_{2}\text{He}$

An alpha particle (He) is emitted which has a mass of 4 and a charge of +2. This means the mass of Po will be 4 less than Ra, and the charge will be 2 less.

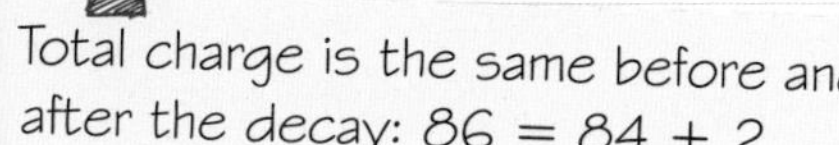

Total charge is the same before and after the decay: 86 = 84 + 2

Total mass is the same before and after the decay: 220 = 216 + 4

Worked example

The activity of a sample of a radioactive substance is shown in the graph.

Use the graph to work out the half-life of the sample.

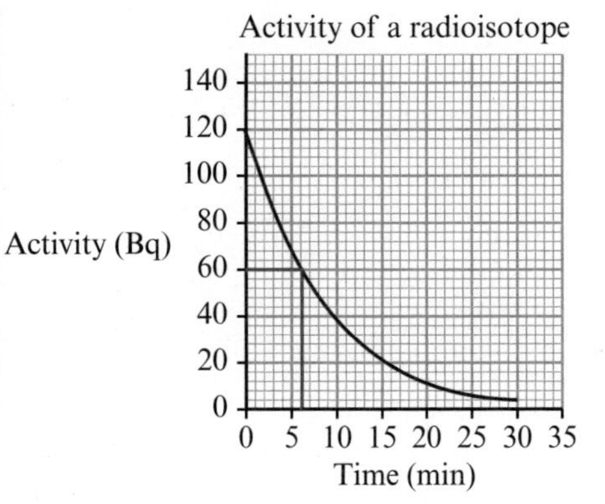

(2 marks)

Half-life is 6 minutes.

1 Bq is 1 nuclear decay per second. Activity can also be given in other units, e.g. counts per minute.

Half of the initial activity is 60 Bq. Draw a horizontal line across to the graph line then down to the time axis.

Read off the value of the half-life.

The initial activity at time = 0 is 120 Bq

You can use any part of the curve that makes it easier to read the values off the graph.

Had a go ☐ Nearly there ☐ Nailed it! ☐

Exam practice

1. Complete these nuclear decay equations.

(a) Beryllium-15 decays by emitting a neutron. **(2 marks)**

$^{15}_{4}Be \rightarrow$ .... $+ n$

(b) Phosphorus-32 decays by emitting a beta-minus particle. **(2 marks)**

$^{32}_{15}P \rightarrow ^{.......}_{.......}S +$ ....

(c) Radon-222 decays by emitting an alpha particle. **(3 marks)**

$^{222}_{.......}Rn \rightarrow ^{.......}_{84}Po +$ ....

(d) Phosphorus-30 decays by emitting a beta-plus particle. **(3 marks)**

$^{.......}_{15}P \rightarrow ^{30}_{.......}Si +$ ....

2. Write a balanced nuclear equation to show each decay.

(a) ^{235}U decays by emitting an alpha particle to form thorium (Th). The atomic number of uranium (U) is 92. **(3 marks)**

(b) Caesium-137 (Cs) decays by emitting a beta-minus particle to form barium (Ba). The atomic number of barium is 56. **(3 marks)**

Knowledge check

The upper number is the mass number or the mass of the nucleus. The lower number is the charge in the nucleus or on the particle.

Go through the nuclear decay equations step by step, as in the example on page 42. Every particle should have two numbers on its left.

Complete each equation by writing the information you have for all three particles. Then balance the mass and charge on both sides.

Exam practice

3. The activity of a sample of a radioactive substance is shown in the graph.

Use the graph to work out the half-life of the sample.

(3 marks)

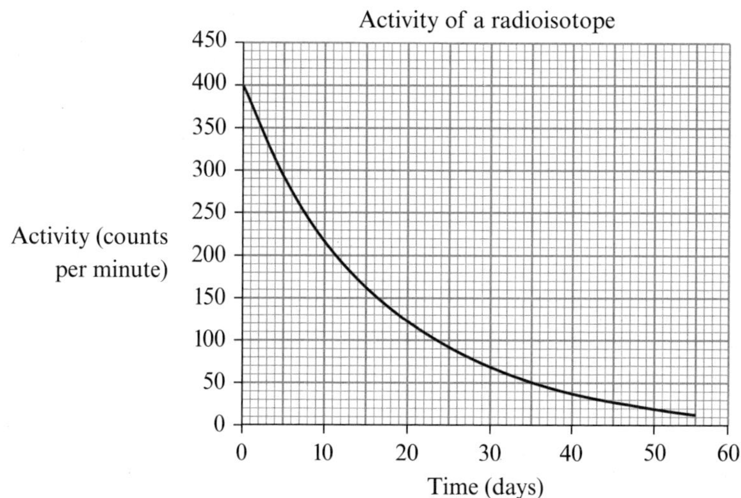

4. The half-life of a radioisotope is 7 years. The initial activity of a sample of the radioisotope is 240 Bq.

Plot a graph to show how the activity of this isotope will change from the time of the first measurement.

(3 marks)

Examiner's hint

Always show your working by drawing lines on the graph. Label clearly what you do.

Maths skills Look at and use the units given on the graph for activity and time. In this case, they are not the SI units of Bq and seconds.

Check your answer by choosing a different starting activity. Does the activity halve in the time you have worked out?

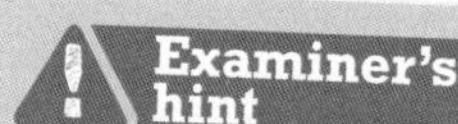

Four points are a suitable number of points to mark on this curve.

83–88

Resistors

What's it all about?

Resistance

The electrical resistance of a component or material is a way of measuring how hard it is for a current to flow through it. The units for resistance are ohms (Ω). Materials with extremely high resistance are insulators. Different conducting materials vary in resistance, and a component or material with any resistance is called a resistor. Resistance is calculated using the equation:

potential difference (V) = current (A) × resistance (Ω) $\quad V = I \times R$

I–V graphs

The graph shows how current flowing through a resistor varies with the potential difference across it.

Across a fixed resistor, the current and potential difference are in direct proportion so the line is straight.

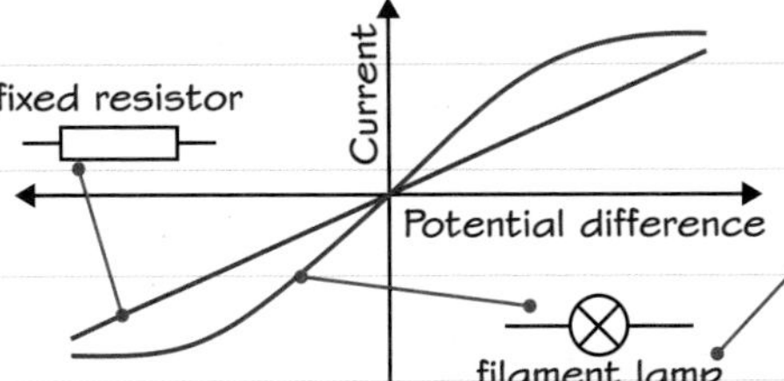

Across a filament lamp the current and potential difference are not in direct proportion, so the line is curved. As the filament gets hot the resistance increases.

Light-dependent resistor (LDR)

The resistance of an LDR decreases as the light intensity (brightness) increases.

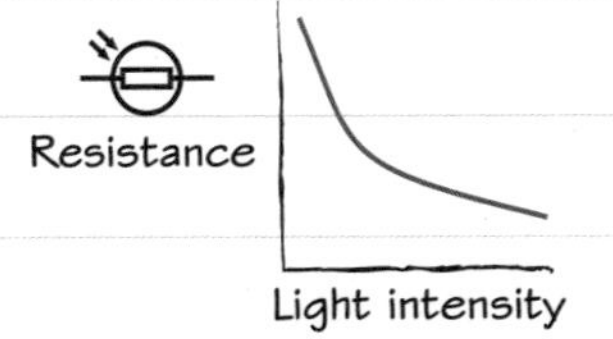

Thermistor

The resistance of a thermistor decreases as the temperature increases.

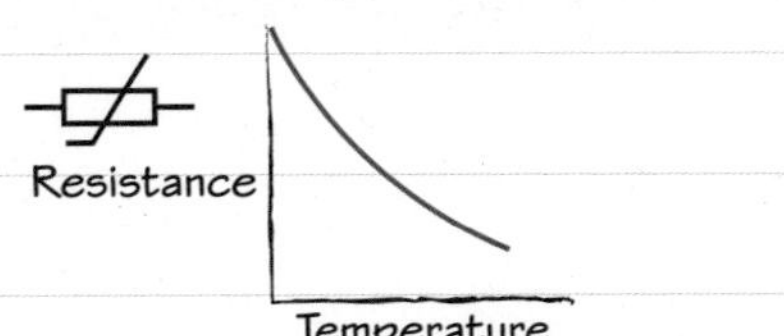

Resistors in series

- One pathway for current.
- Total resistance increased.
- Potential difference shared between the resistors but not equally.
- Greater potential difference across resistors with higher resistance.

6 V
P 2 Ω
Q 10 Ω

Resistors in parallel

- More pathways for current.
- Total resistance is less than the resistance of the individual resistors.

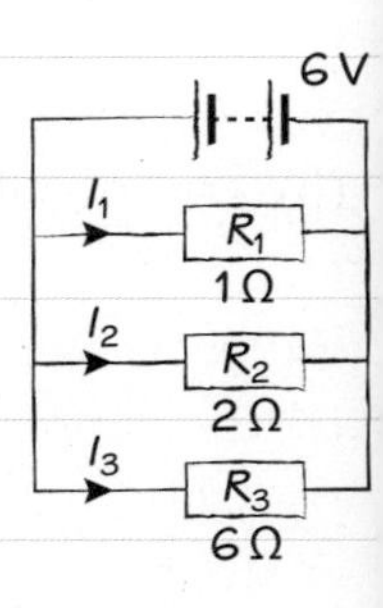

Worked example

Two 4 Ω resistors are connected together in a circuit. The power supply voltage is 12 V. The current measured in series with the power supply is 6 A.

Show that the resistors are connected in parallel. **(2 marks)**

From $V = I \times R$, the resistance in the circuit is calculated as:

$$R = \frac{12}{6} = 2\,\Omega$$

If the resistors were in series, the total resistance would be $4 + 4 = 8\,\Omega$

So the resistors must be connected in parallel.

A 'Show that' question means you need to give some evidence to justify the statement. In this case, you need to do calculations to show the resistors are not in series (and therefore must be in parallel).

Worked example

There is a heating effect when a current flows in a resistor.

(a) Give one use of this heating effect. **(1 mark)**

In a hairdryer.

(b) Explain what causes the heating effect when a current flows in a resistor. **(3 marks)**

A current is the movement of free electrons through a lattice of positive ions. As the electrons flow they collide with the ions, transferring energy to them. This energy transfer causes the resistor to warm up as the ions vibrate more.

Learn a few advantages and disadvantages of the heating effect; you can also use ideas from your own knowledge.

Write your answer in a systematic way so that one point follows on from the next. There are three marks for this question so write three separate points.

Worked example

(a) Sketch a graph to show how current varies with potential difference for a diode. **(1 mark)**

Current

Potential difference

(b) Describe the resistance of a diode using the graph. **(2 marks)**

When the potential difference is in the negative direction, the resistance is very high so current does not flow. In the opposite direction, the resistance is constant once the potential difference reaches a threshold value.

A sketch graph does not need scales on the axes.

Maths skills

When describing a graph, look at all parts of it and note any changes in gradient.

Exam practice

1. A current flows through a filament lamp.

(a) Explain the effect of the current on the wire in the filament lamp. **(3 marks)**

State the effect a current has on a wire, then give the physics behind the effect.

(b) Draw a circuit diagram that could be used to find the relationship between current and potential difference for a filament lamp. **(3 marks)**

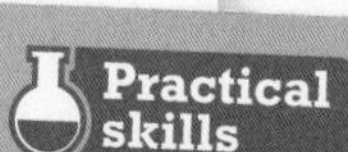

This is a core practical. You need to measure both current and potential difference.

2. Two resistors are arranged in a circuit as shown in the diagram.

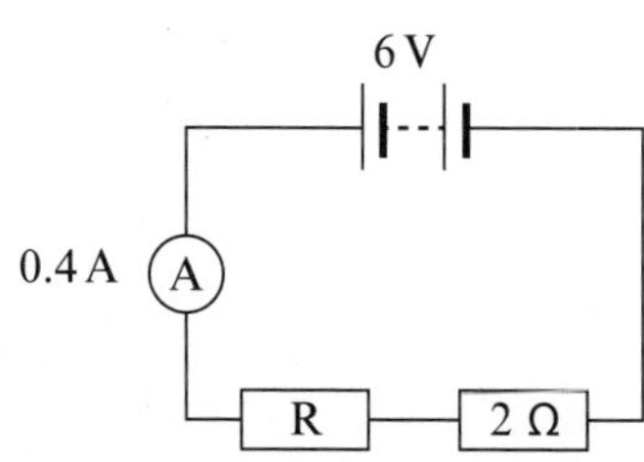

First calculate the total resistance of the circuit. Then find the contribution made by fixed resistor *R*.

Calculate the resistance of resistor *R*. **(3 marks)**

R = ... Ω

Exam practice

3. Two resistors, R_1 and R_2, are arranged in a circuit as shown in the diagram.

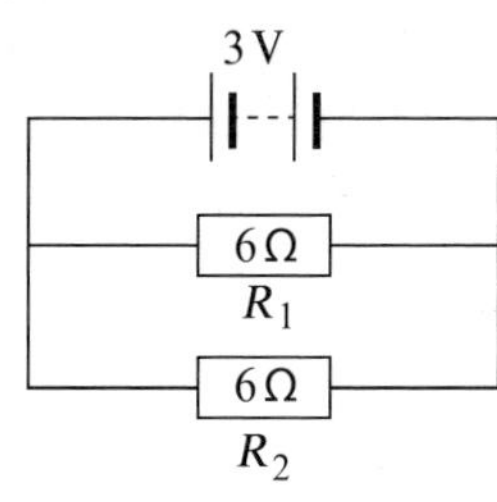

In parallel circuits, the voltage across each resistor in parallel is the same as the voltage of the power supply.

(a) Calculate the current flowing through R_1. **(2 marks)**

R_1 = ... Ω

(b) Calculate the total current supplied by the power supply. **(2 marks)**

Current = ... A

4. Give two ways to reduce energy loss in wires carrying a fixed current. **(2 marks)**

Lower resistance means less energy transfer so think about ways to reduce resistance in wires. Your answers should be comparative.

5. Explain why a thermistor is used in a fire alarm. **(2 marks)**

Think about the effect of temperature on a thermistor and how this could be used in a fire alarm.

102, 104, 105

Transformers

What's it all about?

Electromagnetic induction

Electromagnetic induction is when a potential difference (voltage) is induced in a wire, causing a current to flow in a circuit. It occurs when:

- a wire is moved in a magnetic field
- there is a changing magnetic field caused by an alternating current.

Transformers

Transformers use electromagnetic induction to increase (step-up) and decrease (step-down) potential differences. They change the potential difference of an alternating current and do not work with a direct current.

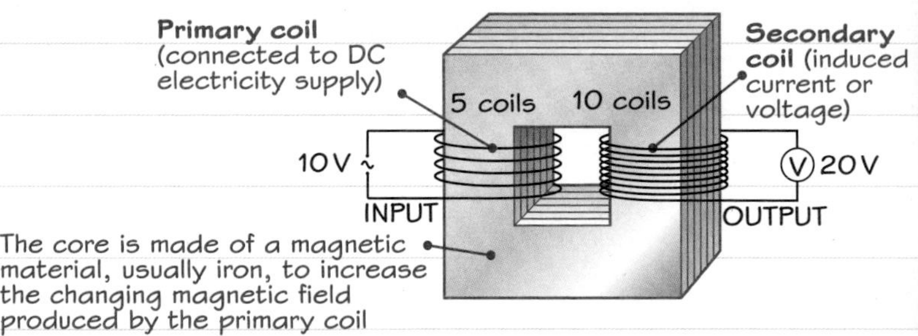

Turns ratio

The relationship between the potential differences in the primary and secondary coils and the turns ratio is given by the equation:

$$\frac{V_p}{V_s} = \frac{N_p}{N_s}$$

Power

If a transformer is assumed to be 100% efficient, the input power is equal to the output power. Remember:

power = potential difference × current

So: $V_p \times I_p = V_s \times I_s$

Transformers and the National Grid

Transformers step up the potential difference to transmit electricity through the National Grid. Increasing the potential difference reduces the current, which reduces unwanted energy transfers from the wires by heating.

These relationships can be considered using the equations:

$P = \frac{E}{t}$ $P = I \times V$ $P = I^2 \times R$

$V_p \times I_p = V_s \times I_s$

Transformers step down the potential difference to safe levels for use in homes and in industry.

Worked example

A transformer has 40 turns on the primary coil and 240 turns on the secondary coil. A potential difference of 20 V is applied across the primary coil.

(a) Calculate the potential difference across the secondary coil. **(3 marks)**

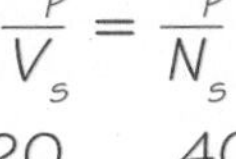

$$\frac{V_p}{V_s} = \frac{N_p}{N_s}$$

$$\frac{20}{V_s} = \frac{40}{240}$$

$$\frac{20}{V_s} = \frac{1}{6}$$

$$V_s = \frac{20 \times 6}{1}$$

$$V_s = 120\,\text{V}$$

(b) Calculate the current in the secondary coil when the current in the primary coil is 15 A. **(3 marks)**

$$V_p \times I_p = V_s \times I_s$$

$$20 \times 15 = 120 \times I_s$$

$$I_s = \frac{20 \times 15}{120}$$

$$I_s = 2.5\,\text{A}$$

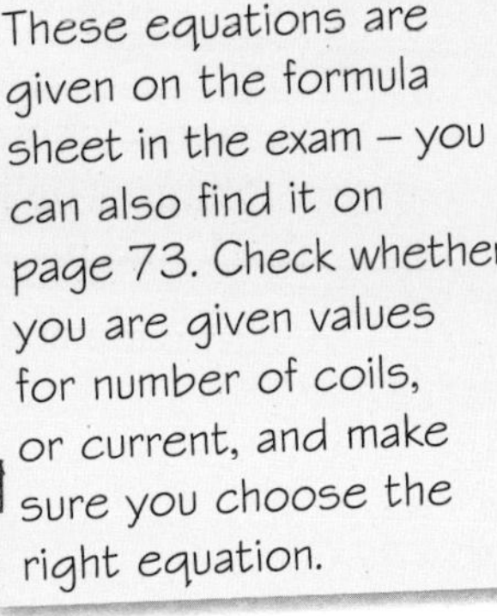

These equations are given on the formula sheet in the exam – you can also find it on page 73. Check whether you are given values for number of coils, or current, and make sure you choose the right equation.

- Substitute known values into the equation.
- Simplify the equation.
- Rearrange the equation to get V_s on its own.
- Calculate the answer, and remember to include the units if they are not given.

Practise rearranging both equations on this page so you can make every value the subject of each equation.

Worked example

Explain the effect of this input current on a transformer.

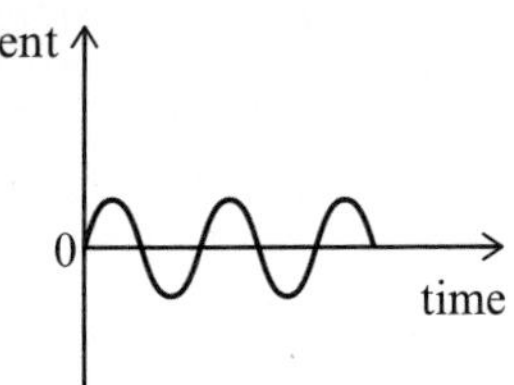

(2 marks)

A changing current creates a changing magnetic field in the primary coil of a transformer. This induces an alternating potential difference and current in the secondary coil.

As well as recognising that the current shown is alternating, you also need to explain how a transformer works.

 Had a go ☐ **Nearly there** ☐ **Nailed it!** ☐

Exam practice

1. (a) A mobile phone charger contains a transformer with 1150 turns on the primary coil. The input voltage is 230 V and the output voltage is 5 V.

Calculate the number of turns on the secondary coil. **(3 marks)**

.... turns

(b) The current in the secondary coil is 1.55 A.

(i) Calculate the current in the primary coil. Give your answer in mA. **(3 marks)**

.... mA

(ii) Give one assumption you have made about transformers in this calculation. **(1 mark)**

Knowledge check

Make sure you understand the physics of the situation before selecting an equation to use.

Maths skills

The value for current is given to 3 sf so give your answer to 3 sf too.

Maths skills

You need to convert between units: 1 A = 1000 mA so multiply amps by 1000 to get mA.

Exam practice

2. Mains electricity is sent from power stations at 400 kV. It is stepped down in a first transformer to 33 kV. Then it is stepped down again in a second transformer to 230 V.

   (a) The turns ratio of a transformer is $N_p : N_s$.
   Explain which transformer has the higher turns ratio. **(3 marks)**

   (b) Explain why transmitting electricity at very high voltages in the National Grid allows the distribution of electrical power to be more efficient. Include equations to support your answer. **(4 marks)**

Knowledge check

Remember what prefixes such as k, M and m stand for.

Examiner's hint

The explanation needs some reasoning which includes calculations to justify your answer.

Examiner's hint

Convert quantities to the same units before you do any calculations.

Examiner's hint

You need to recall the equation linking power, current and resistance, and select the transformer power equation.

Synoptic link

Think about what efficiency means in physics.

93–96

Static electricity

What's it all about?

Static electricity occurs when electric charges are transferred to or from the surface of an **insulator**. This causes the insulator to gain a **negative charge** or a **positive charge**.

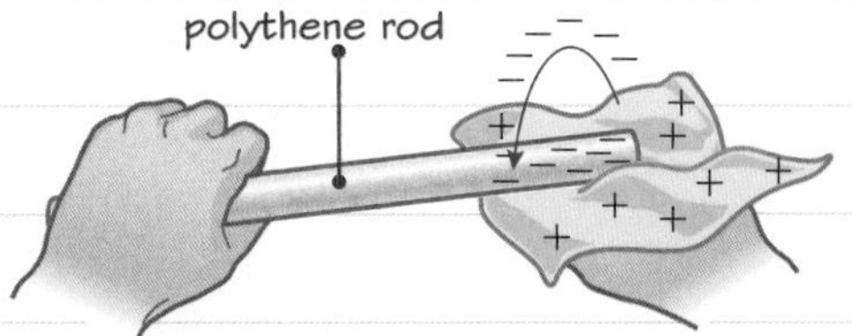

Negatively charged insulator

It is **always electrons** that are transferred when insulators become charged by friction.

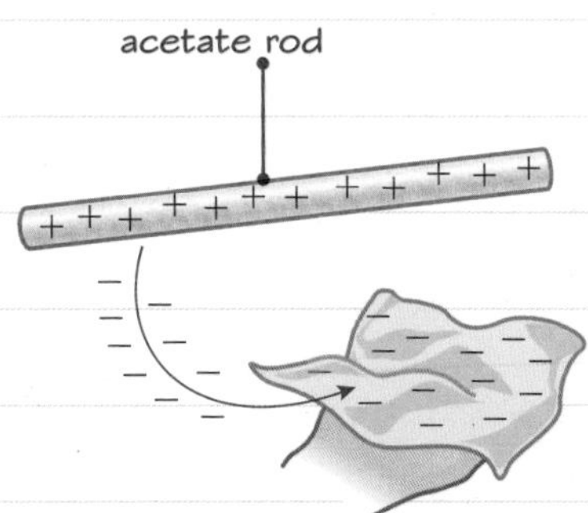

Positively charged insulator

Electrostatic induction

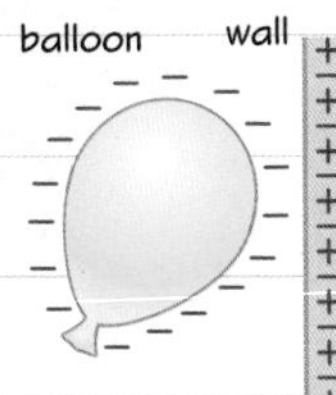

The balloon has a negative charge.

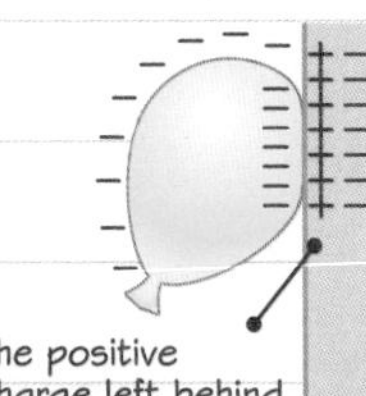

The electrons in the wall are repelled and move away.

The positive charge left behind (the **induced charge**) attracts the negative charge on the balloon.

Charges are not transferred from the balloon, however the positive charges on the wall have been induced. This is called charging by induction.

Like charges **repel** and unlike charges **attract**.

Electric fields

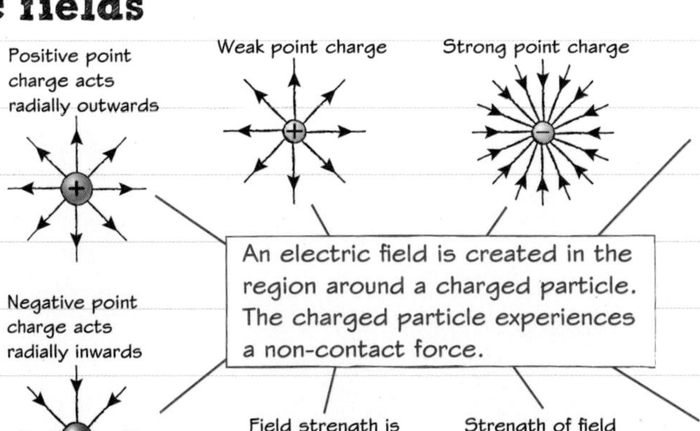

Worked example

Explain how you can get an electric shock when getting out of a car.

(4 marks)

Clothes are insulators.
Friction between your clothes and the car seat transfers electrons onto you. As you touch a metal or conducting part of the car (while getting out), the electrons transfer to the earth and you feel a shock.

Choose appropriate key words when describing electrostatic phenomena: insulator; friction; electron; transfer; charge; negative; positive; electric field; attract; repel; induction.

Worked example

Explain how electron movement causes lightning between clouds and the ground. **(4 marks)**

Friction between particles inside clouds causes electron transfer.
The electrons gather at the bottom of the cloud and repel electrons in the ground.
The electrons in the cloud transfer to the ground in a flash of lightning.

There are four marks for this question so write four steps to explain how lightning between clouds and the ground is caused by electron movement.

Worked example

Fuel hoses in petrol stations are earthed.

A build-up of charge can also be dangerous in areas where there is a high oxygen concentration.

Explain why the fuel hose used to put petrol in a car is earthed. **(3 marks)**

As the fuel flows down the hose, friction causes a charge to build up.
This charge needs to be removed and conducted to earth to avoid a discharge of electrons, which could cause a spark and ignite vaporised fuel.

Exam practice

1. A TV screen is positively charged.

Explain why TV screens get very dusty. **(3 marks)**

This is electrostatic induction. A charged object (TV screen) attracts uncharged objects (dust particles) by inducing a charge in them. The dust particles can move easily as they are small and light.

2. (a) Define an electric field. **(1 mark)**

(b) Complete the diagrams to show the electric fields. **(2 marks)**

Electric field is a vector quantity.

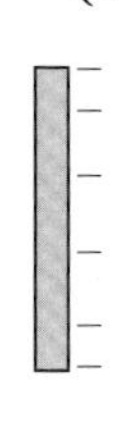

3. (a) A balloon is made from an insulating material.

Explain how a balloon can be negatively charged using a dry cloth. **(3 marks)**

Use correct terms to explain the physics of the situation, such as friction, charges, electrons.

Exam practice

(b) Explain how a negatively charged balloon near to a head of hair makes the hair stand on end. **(3 marks)**

Knowledge check

This question is about induction so explain each stage to show how this happens.

4. The diagram shows an electrostatic precipitator in a chimney.

Explain how the electrostatic precipitator is used to remove smoke particles as they rise up the chimney. **(4 marks)**

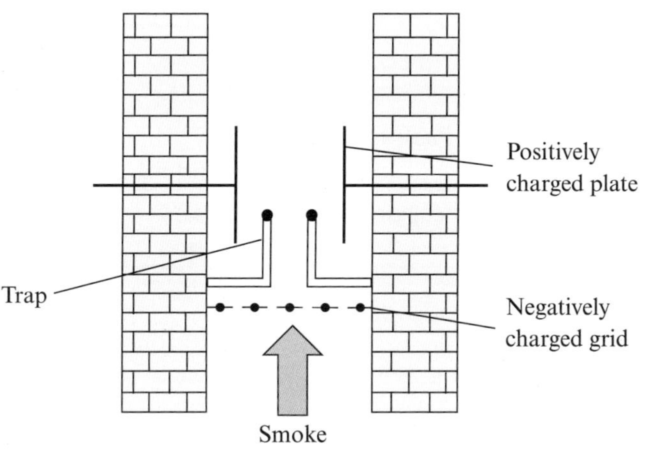

Examiner's hint

You are asked to **explain** how the precipitator works, not just describe it. This requires detail about the physics of static electricity.

Specific heat capacity and specific latent heat

What's it all about?

Specific heat capacity

This is the thermal energy transferred to change the temperature of 1 kg of a material by 1 °C.

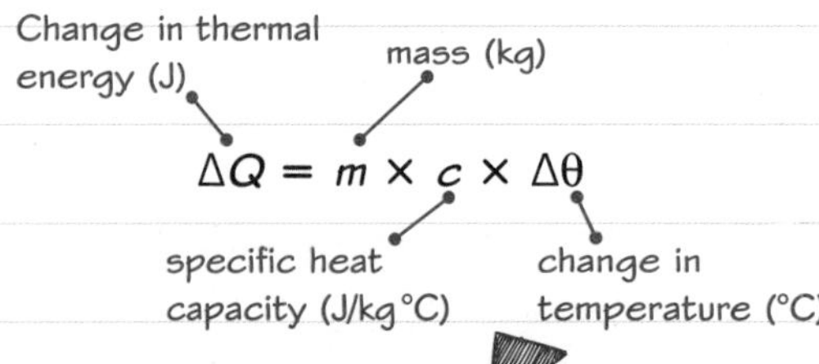

Be careful! Do not confuse specific latent heat with specific heat capacity. Specific latent heat calculations never involve a change in temperature because changes of state always occur at a constant temperature.

Specific latent heat

This is the energy transferred to change 1 kg of a material from one state of matter to another.

You can use this equation to calculate the thermal energy required:

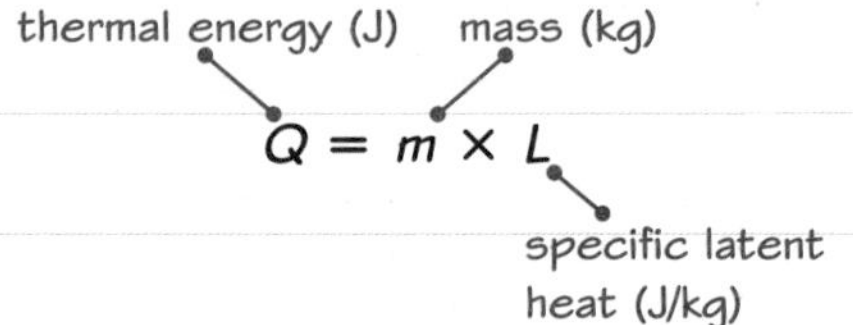

There are two values:

Specific latent heat	Change of state	When it happens
Fusion	Solid and liquid	Melting or freezing
Vaporisation	Liquid and gas	Boiling or condensing

Temperature–time graphs

This graph shows the temperature of a solid substance heated at a steady rate until it becomes a gas.

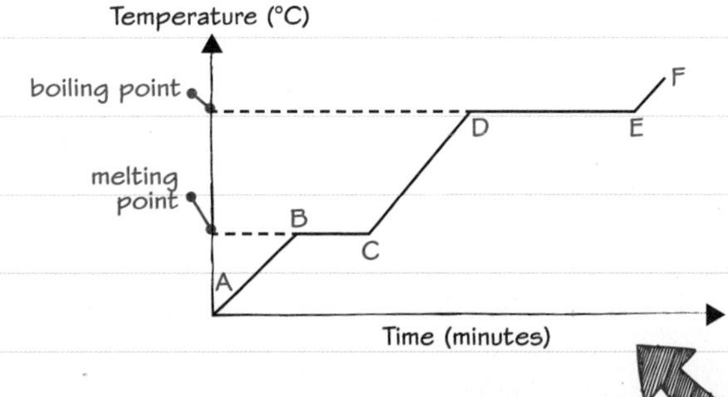

A–B: solid heating
B–C: solid melting
C–D: liquid heating
D–E: liquid vaporising
E–F: gas heating

This substance takes longer to vaporise then it does to melt. It will have a higher specific latent heat of vaporisation than fusion as the same amount of the substance takes more energy to vaporise than it does to melt.

Worked example

890 J of thermal energy is transferred to 0.50 kg of a material. Calculate the temperature change if the specific heat capacity of the material is 76 J/kg °C. **(3 marks)**

> Check whether you need to convert any units.

$\Delta Q = m \times c \times \Delta\theta$

$890 = 0.50 \times 76 \times \Delta\theta$

$890 = 38 \times \Delta\theta$

$\Delta\theta = \frac{890}{38} = 23\,°\text{C}$

> Substitute in the values given; simplify the calculation; rearrange to make $\Delta\theta$ the subject; calculate answer.

> 23.42 °C is closer to the calculated answer, but as the values in the question are given to 2 sf, you should give your answer to the same.

Worked example

Substance 1 and substance 2 are both liquids at room temperature. 0.4 kg of each liquid is heated from room temperature using the same heat source. The diagram shows the temperature–time graph for both substances.

Temperature
Substance 1
Substance 2
Time

> The flat part of each graph line shows when a change of state happens at a constant temperature.

(a) Substance 1 has a higher boiling point and a lower specific latent heat of vaporisation than substance A. Explain how this is shown by the graph. **(2 marks)**

The flat part of each line shows the boiling point and this is higher for substance 1 than for substance 2. The length of the flat section shows the time taken to boil; substance 1 takes less time to boil than substance 2. As the mass and energy supplied are the same, the specific latent heat of vaporisation of substance 1 is lower, as it takes less thermal energy to boil it.

> Look at the time axis to see how long the same mass of each substance takes to melt. They are being provided with thermal energy at the same rate.

(b) It took 1250 J to boil 0.40 kg of substance 1. Calculate the specific latent heat of vaporisation of substance 1. Give your answer correct to 2 significant figures. **(3 marks)**

$Q = m \times L$

$1250 = 0.40 \times L$

$L = \frac{1250}{0.40} = 3100\,\text{J/kg}$

> **Maths skills**
> You will get a mark for giving your answer to the required number of significant figures.

Exam practice

1. A student determines the specific heat capacity of water. The water is heated with an electric heater. The energy transferred to the water is measured with a joulemeter.

The student records these measurements.

Temperature rise = 15 °C

Mass of water = 0.35 kg

Energy transferred = 24 000 J

(a) Calculate the specific heat capacity of water using the student's results. **(3 marks)**

.... J/kg °C

You need to select and apply an equation from the formula sheet on page 73.

(b) Explain how this method could be improved to get a more accurate value of the specific heat capacity of water. **(2 marks)**

As this is an 'explain' question, as well as suggesting an improvement, you must also give the reason why this would make the result more accurate.

(c) Determine how much energy is released when 0.35 kg of water cools by 8 °C. Use your calculated value for the specific heat capacity of water. **(2 marks)**

Knowledge check

The energy change will be the same for both warming and cooling the same mass of a substance by the same temperature change.

.... J

Exam practice

2. A student puts some water into a freezer.

The water has an initial temperature of 20 °C.

The temperature of the freezer is −5 °C.

(a) Sketch a graph of temperature against time to show how the temperature of the water would change as it cools down to freezer temperature. **(2 marks)**

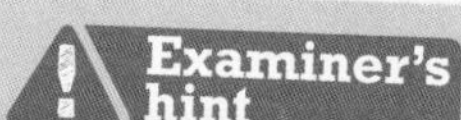

For a graph, 'sketch' means draw the graph line and unscaled axes with labelled features. You can draw freehand but it is a good idea to use a ruler for straight lines.

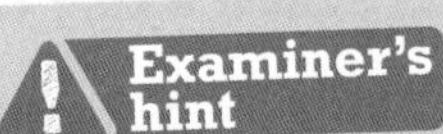

You are given values for temperature so add them to your graph. They do not have to be to scale.

(b) Define the specific latent heat of fusion. **(1 mark)**

(c) The ice formed has a mass of 150 g. The specific latent heat of fusion is 334 000 J/kg for water.

Calculate how much thermal energy is needed to re-melt the ice. **(2 marks)**

Convert g to kg by dividing by 1000.

.... J

113, 118, 119

Pressure

What's it all about?

Pressure is the force acting per unit area, measured at right angles to the area. Pressure is measured in pascals (Pa):

1 Pa = 1 N/m^2

You can use this equation to calculate pressure:

pressure (Pa) = force normal to surface (N) ÷ area of surface (m^2)

$$P = \frac{F}{A}$$

Pressure in fluids

Fluids (liquids and gases) exert pressure. The pressure depends on the depth and density of the fluid.

The pressure in a fluid causes a force that is normal to any surface. This means that the force is at right angles or perpendicular to the surface on which it acts.

Pressure in gases

You can use this equation to calculate the pressure or volume of gases for a fixed mass of gas at a constant temperature:

$$P_1 \times V_1 = P_2 \times V_2$$

Pressure, depth and density

The pressure exerted due to a liquid will increase with depth. This is because the further down you go, the greater the volume, and weight, of liquid above. A liquid with a higher density will exert more pressure than the same volume of another liquid in the same shape of container with a lower density.

You can calculate the pressure due to a liquid using the equation:

pressure due to a column of liquid (Pa) = height of column (m) × density of liquid (kg/m^3) × gravitational field strength (N/kg)

$$P = h \times \rho \times g$$

Atmospheric pressure

The atmosphere is like a very high column of air above our bodies. This means the atmosphere will exert a pressure due to its weight, which acts normal to an area, *A*.

The further up you go in the Earth's atmosphere, the less air there is above you. Less air means less weight of air so less pressure.

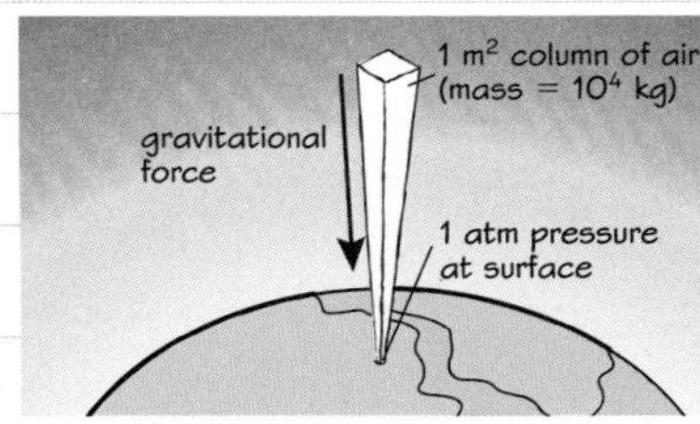

The total pressure acting due to a fluid in an open system depends on the pressure from the fluid **and** atmospheric pressure. A piston is an example of a closed system not open to the air.

Worked example

The diagram shows a piston.

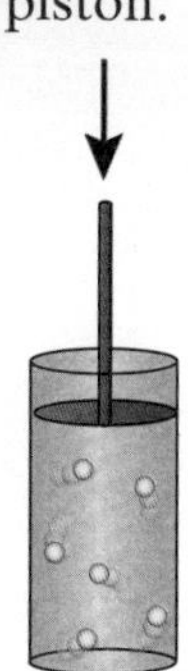

(a) The area of the piston is 35 cm².

Calculate the force on the piston when the pressure is 120 000 Pa. **(4 marks)**

$35\,\text{cm}^2 = 35 \div 10000 = 0.0035\,\text{m}^2$

Use $P = \frac{F}{A}$

$120000 = \frac{F}{0.0035}$

$F = 120000 \times 0.0035$

$F = 420\,\text{N}$

(b) The volume of the trapped gas in the piston is 73 cm³ at a pressure of 100 kPa.

Calculate the volume of the trapped gas when the pressure is increased to 120 kPa. Assume the temperature is constant. **(3 marks)**

$P_1 = 100\,\text{kPa}$, $V_1 = 73\,\text{cm}^3$, $P_2 = 120\,\text{kPa}$

Use $P_1 \times V_1 = P_2 \times V_2$

$100\,\text{kPa} \times 73\,\text{cm}^3 = 120\,\text{kPa} \times V_2$

$7300 = 120 \times V_2$

$V_2 = \frac{100 \times 73}{120} = \frac{7300}{120}$

$V_2 = 61\,\text{cm}^3$ (to 2 sf)

Start by writing out all the quantities.

Maths skills

Divide the area by 10 000 (100 × 100) to convert cm² to m².

Recall the equation $P = \frac{F}{A}$ and substitute the values.

Select the equation $P_1V_1 = P_2V_2$ and substitute the values.

Maths skills

This equation and the transformers equation are the only ones on the formula sheet with the format WX = YZ so make sure you know how to rearrange them.

Pressure does not need to be converted from kPa to Pa here because the kPa on either side of the equation cancel each other out.

Give your answer to the smallest number of significant figures used in the question. If the initial volume was given as 73.0 cm³, you would put 60.8 cm³ as your answer instead of rounding up to 61 cm³.

Exam practice

1. The diagram shows part of a car braking system which is filled with a fluid.

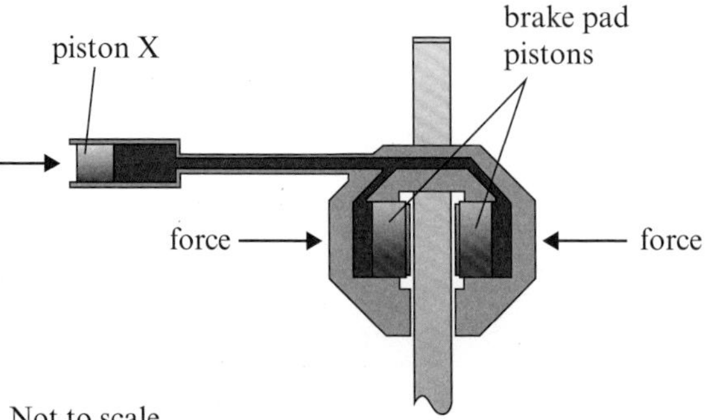

(a) The force on piston X is 104 N.

The area of piston X is 8 cm^2.

The area of each brake pad piston is 25 cm^2.

Calculate the force exerted by each brake pad. **(3 marks)**

.... N

(b) Piston X moves 0.0675 m.

Calculate the distance moved by each brake pad piston. **(4 marks)**

.... m

Knowledge check

The fluid in a braking system cannot be compressed, so the same pressure is transmitted throughout the fluid.

Knowledge check

You need to be able to recall and use $P = \frac{F}{A}$.

Maths skills

The area units are the same so they cancel each other out. This means there is no need to convert cm^2 into m^2 in this example.

Remember there are two brake pad pistons.

Synoptic link

You need to use your knowledge of work done.

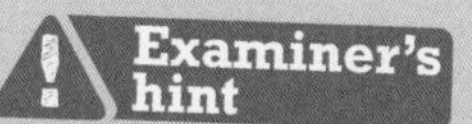

Examiner's hint

Show each stage of the calculation, as marks can be awarded for working even if your answer is wrong.

Exam practice

2. The diagram shows two identical containers with a hole in the side. They are filled with different liquids, 1 and 2.

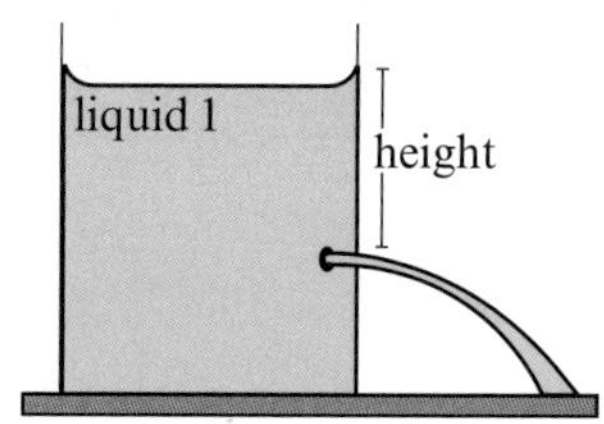

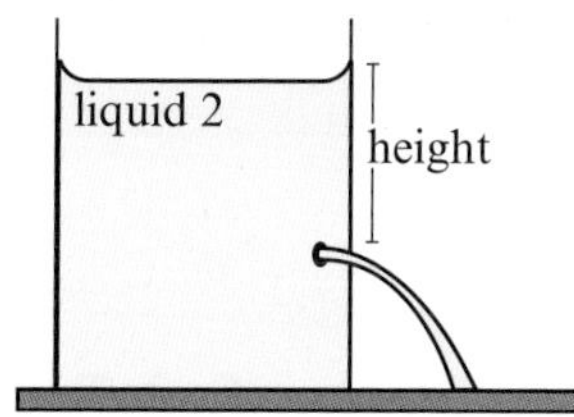

(a) Explain what this diagram shows about the densities of liquid 1 and liquid 2. **(3 marks)**

(b) The pressure due to liquid 2 at the hole is 4450 Pa when the height is 0.5 m.

Calculate the density of liquid 2.

(gravitational field strength (g) = 10 N/kg) **(3 marks)**

.... kg m^3

3. A car tyre has a volume of 0.0025 m^3.

The pressure needed inside the tyre is 220 000 Pa.

Calculate the volume of air needed to pump up the tyre.

Atmospheric pressure = 100 000 Pa.

Assume the temperature of the air inside the tyre is the same as the temperature of the air outside the tyre. **(3 marks)**

.... m^3

Examiner's hint

The equations used on this page are given on the formula sheet with the exam paper. You can also find them on page 73.

Two values are given for pressure. Make sure you match them with the correct volumes.

Answers

Extended response questions

In your exam, your answers to 6-mark questions will be marked on how well you present and organise your response, not just on the scientific content. Your responses should contain most or all of the points given in the answers below, but you should also make sure that you show how the points link to each other, and structure your response in a clear and logical way.

2–5. Knowledge check

1. C
2. C
3. A
4. force = mass × acceleration
5. C
6. C
7. B
8. longitudinal
9. B
10. ultrasound waves
11. energy
12. B
13. B
14. B
15. An early model of the atom
16. A proton becomes a neutron plus a positron
17. Mercury, Venus, Earth, Mars, Jupiter, Saturn, Uranus, Neptune
18. C
19. It changes direction, speed or both
20. C
21. newton metre, Nm
22. 
23. coulomb, C
24. The rate of flow of charge
25. D
26. Thermal
27. B
28. C
29. B
30. earthing
31. National Grid
32. sublimation
33. A
34. D
35. 3.18×10^{-3}
36. B
37. D
38. C

6–9. Distance, speed and time

1. (a) $1.2 = \frac{(9-5)}{t}$ **(1)**

$t = \frac{4}{1.2}$ **(1)**

$t = 3.3\,\text{s}$ **(1)**

(b) $9^2 - 5^2 = 2 \times 1.2 \times x$ **(1)**

$56 = 2.4 \times x$

$x = \frac{56}{2.4}$ **(1)**

$x = 23\,\text{m}$ **(1)**

2. (a) Correctly identify points to calculate areas: (0,0), (20,35) and (120,35) **(1)**

Area when speeding up = $0.5 \times 20 \times 35$
= 350 m **(1)**

Area at constant velocity = $(120 - 20) \times 35$
= 3500 m **(1)**

So the distance travelled at constant speed is 10 times further. **(1)**

(b) acceleration = change in velocity ÷ time taken

$= \frac{0 - 35}{160 - 120}$ **(1)**

$= \frac{-35}{40}$ **(1)**

$= -0.88\,\text{m/s}^2$ (accept $0.875\,\text{m/s}^2$) **(1)**

10–13. Force, acceleration and circular motion

1. (a) Using two light gates means that acceleration can be calculated **(1)** using:

$a = \frac{(v-u)}{t}$ **(1)**

(b) The pulling force must be the same each time (as the mass of the trolley is the independent variable). **(1)**

(c) The string needs to be long enough to allow the masses to hit the floor while the trolley is still on the ramp **(1)** but not so long that the masses hit the floor before the trolley has travelled through both light gates. **(1)**

(d) Protect people/floor from falling masses/equipment falling from the bench. **(1)**

2. (a) The friction between the bicycle tyres and the track. **(1)**

   (b) Speed is a scalar quantity so it only has magnitude. Velocity is a vector quantity so it has both magnitude and direction. **(1)** The direction of the cyclist is changing so the velocity is also changing. **(1)**

3. The lorry has a higher (inertial) mass **(1)** so the same force will produce a smaller deceleration/acceleration **(1)** so the lorry will take more time/travel a further distance before stopping. **(1)**

   An alternative answer would be: The lorry has a larger momentum **(1)**. The same force will take more time to change a larger momentum (as force = rate of change of momentum) **(1)**. So, the lorry will take more time/travel a further distance before stopping. **(1)**

4. Use $F = m \times a$ and convert 210 g to kg:

$$210\,\text{g} = \frac{210}{1000} = 0.21\,\text{kg}$$

$$3.4 = 0.21 \times a \ \mathbf{(1)}$$

$$a = \frac{3.4}{0.21} \ \mathbf{(1)}$$

$$= 16\,\text{m/s}^2 \ \mathbf{(1)}$$

14–17. Momentum and collisions

1. $F = \dfrac{mv - mu}{t}$

$$= \frac{(2500 \times 25) - (2500 \times 20)}{0.5} \ \mathbf{(1)}$$

$$= \frac{50\,000 - 62\,500}{0.5} = \frac{-12\,500}{0.5} \ \mathbf{(1)}$$

$$= -25\,000\,\text{N} \ \mathbf{(1)}$$

2. (a) momentum = mass × velocity

$$= 0.17 \times 0.82 \ \mathbf{(1)}$$

$$= 0.14\,\text{kg m/s} \ \mathbf{(1)}$$

   (b) momentum before collision = momentum after collision

$$0.14 = (0.17 \times 0.10) + (m \times 0.74) \ \mathbf{(1)}$$

$$0.14 = 0.017 + (0.74 \times m)$$

$$0.14 - 0.017 = 0.74 \times m \ \mathbf{(1)}$$

$$0.123 = 0.74 \times m$$

$$m = \frac{0.123}{0.74} = 0.17\,\text{kg} \ \mathbf{(1)}$$

3. $F = \dfrac{mv - mu}{t}$

   A crumple zone increases the time taken for the collision **(1)** which reduces the deceleration $\dfrac{v - u}{t}$ **(1)** and hence also reduces the force on the car (compared with having no crumple zone). **(1)**

4. (a) Force is a vector quantity **(1)** and this force acts in the opposite direction to the motion of the bicycle. **(1)**

   (b) $F = \dfrac{mv - mu}{t}$

$$-1700 = \frac{m(0 - 6.0)}{0.30} \ \mathbf{(1)}$$

$$-1700 = -20 \times m$$

$$m = \frac{-1700}{-20} \ \mathbf{(1)}$$

$$m = 85\,\text{kg} \ \mathbf{(1)}$$

5. Use momentum before collision = momentum after collision

$$0.30 \times 0.20 = (0.30 + 0.10) \times v \ \mathbf{(1)}$$

$$0.06 = 0.40 \times v$$

$$v = \frac{0.06}{0.40} \ \mathbf{(1)}$$

$$= 0.15\,\text{m/s} \ \mathbf{(1)}$$

18–21. Force diagrams

1. Both arrows correct **(1)**

2.5 N
normal reaction

2.5 N
weight

2. (a) **(1)** for each correct arrow.

upwards force 20 N

wind force 8 N

   (b)

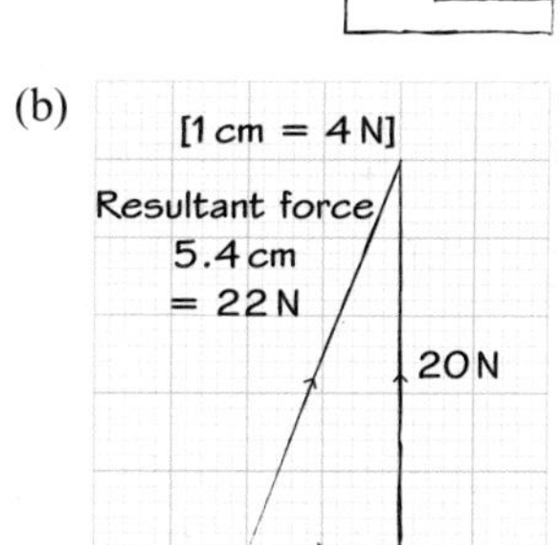

Drawn 8 N and 20 N **(1)**

22N **(1)**

3. 30 N drawn at 65° **(1)**; horizontal force labelled 15 N **(1)**; vertical force labelled 26 N **(1)**

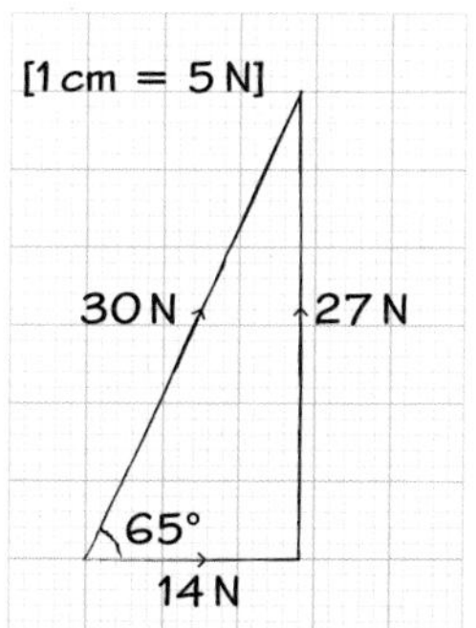

4. (a) Reaction force of child on slide and reaction force of slide on child **(1)**

(b) **(1)**

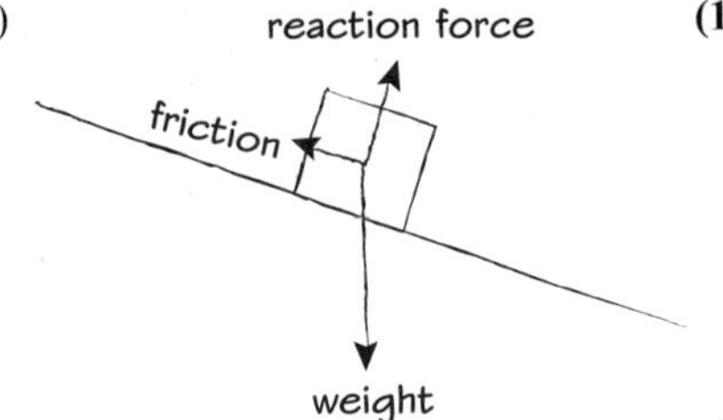

5. 70 N line at 40° **(1)**; vertical value 44 N **(1)**; horizontal value 52 N **(1)**

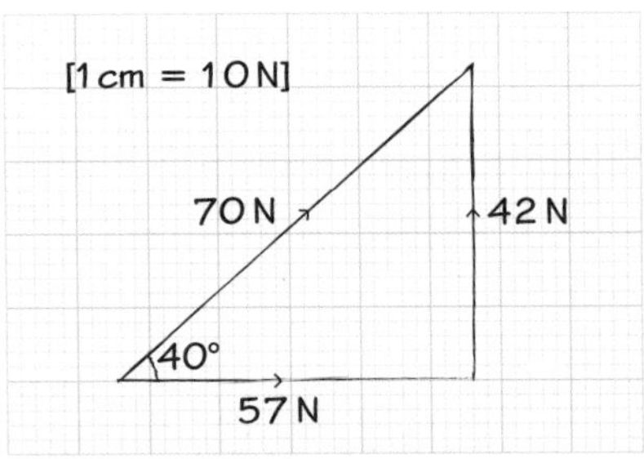

22–25. Rotational forces

1. clockwise moment = anticlockwise moment

$350 \times 1.5 = 300 \times d$ **(1)**

$525 = 300 \times d$ **(1)**

$d = \frac{525}{300} = 1.75\,\text{m}$ **(1)**

2. (a) The clockwise moment around the point where the mobile hangs is equal to the anticlockwise moment. **(1)**

(b) sum of anticlockwise moments = sum of clockwise moments

moment of a force = force × distance normal to the direction of the force

$20\,\text{cm} = \frac{20}{100} = 0.2\,\text{m}$

distance of star from pivot

$= 0.3 + 0.2 = 0.5\,\text{m}$

$60 \times 0.5 = (20 \times 0.3)$ **(1)** +
(mass of star × 0.5) **(1)**

30 = 6 + (mass of star × 0.5)

mass of star $= \frac{30 - 6}{0.5}$ **(1)**

mass of star = 48 g **(1)**

3. The smaller gear wheel will turn 5 times anticlockwise. **(1)**

4. clockwise moment = anticlockwise moment

moment = force × perpendicular distance

clockwise moment = 320 × 0.30 = 96 Nm **(1)**

anticlockwise moment = $80 \times d$ = 96 Nm **(1)**

$d = \frac{96}{80} = 1.2\,\text{m}$ **(1)**

5. clockwise moment = anticlockwise moment

moment = force × perpendicular distance

clockwise moment = 24 × 1.5 = 36 Nm **(1)**

anticlockwise moment = $F \times 0.3$ = 36 Nm **(1)**

$F = \frac{36}{0.3} = 120\,\text{N}$

A force larger than 120N **(1)** is needed to pull the fish from the water.

26–29. Radiation and temperature

1. (a) The hotter the object, the shorter the wavelength of the radiation emitted. **(1)**

(b) infrared radiation **(1)**

(c)

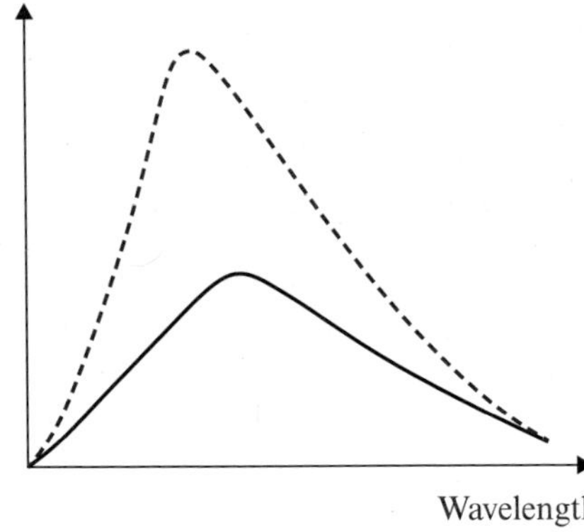

higher peak intensity **(1)**; wavelength shifted left at peak **(1)**

2. The temperature rises because the average power the heater absorbs is greater than the average power it radiates. **(1)** As the temperature increases, the amount of radiation emitted increases. **(1)** At constant temperature, the heater absorbs and radiates energy at the same rate. **(1)**

3. (a) (i) The container cools down as it radiates heat **(1)** more quickly than it absorbs it **(1)**.

(ii) The temperature is constant so the rates of absorption and radiation are equal. **(1)**

(b)

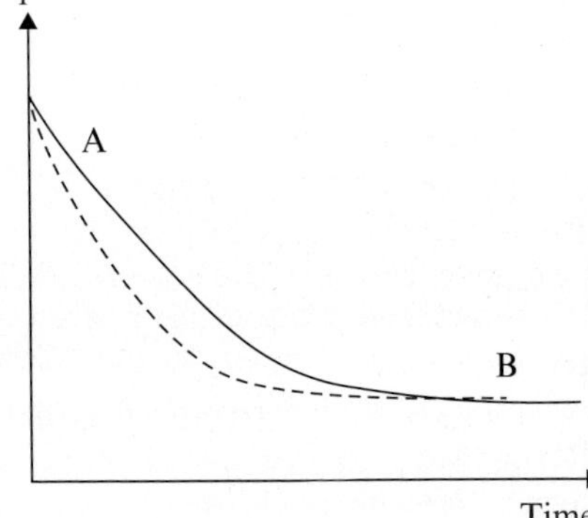

same initial and final temperatures **(1)**; graph curves more steeply and levels off more quickly **(1)**

4. (a) The different colours show where radiation of different IR wavelengths **(1)** has been emitted by parts of the animal at different temperatures **(1)**.

(b) $v = f \times \lambda$

$12\,\mu\text{m} = 12 \times 10^{-6}\,\text{m}$ **(1)**

$3 \times 10^8 = f \times 12 \times 10^{-6}$ **(1)**

$f = \frac{3 \times 10^8}{12 \times 10^{-6}}$ **(1)**

$f = 2.5 \times 10^{13}\,\text{Hz}$ **(1)**

30–33. Speed and uses of sound

1. (a) 21 kHz **(1)**

(b) The ultrasound waves are reflected back to the boat from a shoal of fish. **(1)** The time taken for the echoes to reach the detector is monitored. **(1)** The time taken and the speed of sound in water can be used to calculate the distance of the fish from the boat. **(1)**

(c) $v = \frac{x}{t}$

$t = 0.02\,\text{s}$ **(1)**

$1500 = \frac{x}{0.02}$ **(1)**

$x = 1500 \times 0.02$ **(1)**

$x = 30\,\text{m}$,

so distance from shoal

$= \frac{30}{2} = 15\,\text{m}$ **(1)**

(d) The ultrasound waves transfer vibrations (through the liquid) **(1)** which shake the dirt off the bike chain. **(1)**

2. (a)

waves bent towards the normal **(1)**

wavelengths shorter/wave fronts closer together than in warm air **(1)**

(b) A bigger change in temperature would cause a greater change in speed/wavelength **(1)** and this would cause a bigger change of direction **(1)**.

(c) $v = f \times \lambda$

f is the same for both air temperatures.

$f = \frac{340}{0.04} = 8500\,\text{Hz}$ **(1)**

$v = 8500 \times 0.035$ **(1)**

$v = 300\,\text{m/s}$ **(1)**

34–37. Energy, power and efficiency

(a) change in GPE $= m \times g \times \Delta h$

$240\,000 = m \times 10 \times 30$ **(1)**

$m = \frac{240\,000}{300}$ **(1)** $= 800$ **(1)** kg

(b) (i) power $= \frac{\text{energy transferred}}{\text{time taken}} = \frac{240\,000}{25}$ **(1)**

power = 9600 **(1)** W **(1)** [or 9.6 **(1)** kW **(1)**]

(ii) There is friction between the wheels and the track/the wheels and axles/the motor is not 100% efficient. **(1)** Some energy will be transferred as thermal energy to the surroundings. **(1)**

(c) KE of car = change in GPE as car drops 20 m

$\frac{1}{2} \times m \times v^2 = m \times g \times \Delta h$

$\frac{1}{2} \times v^2 = 10 \times 20$ **(1)**

$v^2 = 400$ **(1)**

$v = \sqrt{400} = 20\,\text{m/s}$ **(1)**

(d) work done = force × distance moved

$270\,000 = F \times 40\,\text{m}$ **(1)**

$F = \frac{270\,000}{40} = 6800\,\text{N}$ or $6.8\,\text{kN}$ **(1)**

38–41. Ionising radiation

1. Gamma rays travel the greatest distance in air and alpha particles travel the shortest distance. **(1)** Alpha particles are stopped by paper but beta particles and gamma rays pass through. **(1)** Alpha and beta particles are stopped by aluminium but gamma rays pass through. **(1)**

2. To gain full marks your answer must be clearly written in a logical structure. It must also show understanding of the scientific ideas involved, including some of the points shown below **(6)**:
   - Irradiation occurs when someone is exposed to a radioactive source.
   - Once the person is removed from the source, they are no longer irradiated.
   - The greater the distance from the source, the weaker the irradiation.
   - The shorter the time spent near a source, the lower the irradiation.
   - Contamination is when radioactive particles come into contact with the body.
   - This contamination continues until all of the radioactive material has decayed.
   - The longer the half-life, the longer this takes.
   - The type of radiation also makes a difference: the more ionising the radiation, the more tissue damage it can cause.
   - Contamination from alpha particles inside the body causes a lot of damage as they are highly ionising.

- Beta particles/gamma rays are more damaging outside the body as they can penetrate the skin (alpha cannot).
- Risks from both irradiation and contamination can be reduced by wearing protective clothing.

3. To gain full marks your answer must be clearly written in a logical structure. It must also show understanding of the scientific ideas involved, including some of the points shown below **(6)**:
   - Smoke detectors work by radiation from the source ionising the air in the smoke detector. This allows a small current to flow between two electrodes.
   - Beta source/nickel-53 has less ionising power (than alpha).
   - Beta source/nickel-53 passes through skin so is unsafe.
   - Gamma source/cobalt-60 is only weakly ionising.
   - Gamma source/cobalt-60 is too penetrating so unsafe.
   - Alpha radiation ionises the air.
   - Alpha is weakly penetrating and stopped by smoke. This decreases the current and sets off the alarm.
   - The isotope should be an alpha emitter with a long half-life. This means the smoke alarm will not need to be changed too often.
   - The alpha source, neptunium-235, could be used, but the half-life is only 396 days.
   - After 1 half-life, the net decline of neptunium-235 is half so the source would need replacing too often. Half of it is gone after 13 months.
   - So, americium-241 is the best choice from these radioisotopes as it emits alpha particles and has a long half-life.

4. (a) Background radiation is the low level ionising radiation that we are exposed to all the time. **(1)** It comes from both natural and man-made sources. **(1)**

   (b) Any two from: radon gas/nuclear power/food and drink/cosmic rays/ground and buildings/medical. **(2)**

42–45. Radioactive decay

1. (a) ${}^{15}_{4}Be \rightarrow {}^{14}_{4}Be + {}^{1}_{0}n$ **(1 for each correct particle) (2)**

   (b) ${}^{32}_{15}P \rightarrow {}^{32}_{16}S + {}^{0}_{-1}e$ **(1 for each correct particle) (2)**

   (c) ${}^{222}_{86}Rn \rightarrow {}^{218}_{84}Po + {}^{4}_{2}He$ **(1 for each correct particle) (3)**

   (d) ${}^{30}_{15}P \rightarrow {}^{30}_{14}Si + {}^{0}_{+1}e$ **(1 for each correct particle) (3)**

2. (a) ${}^{235}_{92}U \rightarrow {}^{231}_{90}Th + {}^{4}_{2}He$ **(1 for each correct particle) (3)**

   (b) ${}^{137}_{55}Cs \rightarrow {}^{137}_{56}Ba + {}^{0}_{-1}e$ **(1 for each correct particle) (3)**

3. Half the initial activity = 200 Bq **(1)**; draw a line on the graph from 200 Bq across to the curve and then down to the time axis **(1)**; half-life = 11.7 ± 0.8 days **(1)** (or similar method)

4. Suitable scale filling at least half of the grid **(1)**; four points plotted ± half a small square **(1)**; points joined with a smooth curve **(1)**

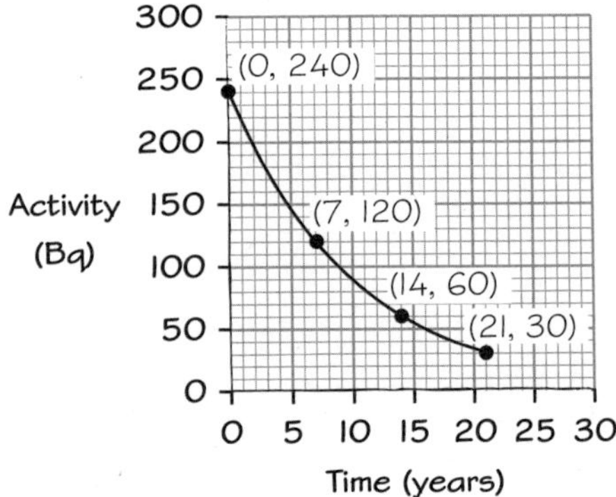

46–49. Resistors

1. (a) The wire gets hot/glows. **(1)** This is because of the collisions between the free-flowing electrons and the positive ions in the wire **(1)** which transfer energy. **(1)**

   (b)

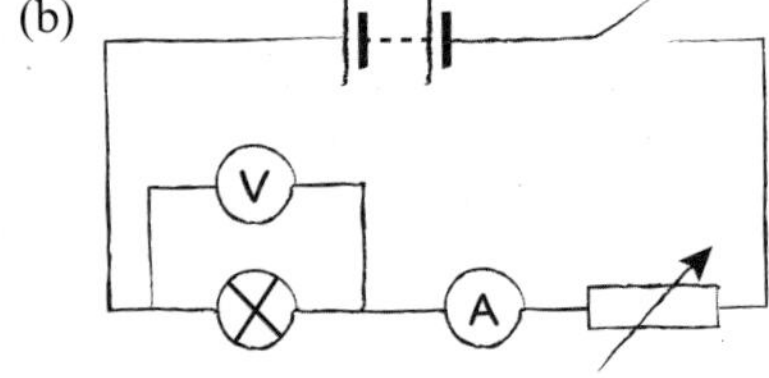

   All symbols correct and in a complete circuit **(1)**; voltmeter across lamp **(1)**; ammeter in series with lamp **(1)**

2. $V = I \times R$

   $6 = 0.4 \times (R + 2)$ **(1)**

   $R + 2 = \frac{6}{0.4} = 15$**(1)**

   $R = 15 - 2 = 13\,\Omega$ **(1)**

3. (a) $V = I \times R$

   $3 = I \times 6$ **(1)**

   $I = \frac{3}{6} = 0.5\,A$ **(1)**

   (b) $R_1 = R_2$ so current through $R_2 = 0.5\,A$

   Current supplied = 0.5 + 0.5 **(1)** = 1 A **(1)**

4. Any two from: Use a metal with lower resistance. use a better conductor; Use thicker wire; Use a shorter wire; Cool the wire to reduce lattic vibration **(2)**

5. The higher the temperature, the lower the resistance. **(1)** So as temperature increases, a current will be able to flow in a circuit with an alarm. **(1)**

50–53. Transformers

1. (a) $\frac{230}{5} = \frac{1150}{N_s}$ **(1)**

$N_s = \frac{1150 \times 5}{230}$ **(1)** = 25 turns **(1)**

(b) (i) $230 \times I_p = 5 \times 1.55$ **(1)**

$5 \times 1.55 = 7.75$

$I_p = \frac{7.75}{230}$ **(1)** = 0.0337 A = 33.7 mA **(1)**

(ii) This calculation assumes that transformers are 100% efficient.

2. (a) Using the equation $\frac{V_p}{V_s} = \frac{N_p}{N_s}$ **(1)** the turns ratio $N_p : N_s$ is equivalent to $V_p : V_s$

In transformer 1: 400 kV : 33 kV = 12 : 1 **(1)**

In transformer 2: 33 kV = 33 000 V; 33 000 V : 230 V = 143 : 1 **(1)**

(so transformer 2 has the higher turns ratio as 143 > 12)

(b) The current in the transmission wires transfers energy to the surroundings by heating. **(1)** The energy transferred by the wires is given by the equation $P = I^2 \times R$. **(1)** So reducing the current reduces the energy transferred/wasted from the wires by heating. **(1)** As $V_p \times I_p = V_s \times I_s$, the current can be reduced (or efficiency can be increased) by increasing the voltage for a given power. **(1)**

54–57. Static electricity

1. The negative charges in dust particles are attracted towards the TV screen and the positive charges are repelled. **(1)** This induces a negative charge in the dust particles. **(1)** The dust particles are then attracted to the positively charged screen. **(1)**

2. (a) An electric field is a region where an electric charge experiences a force. **(1)**

(b)

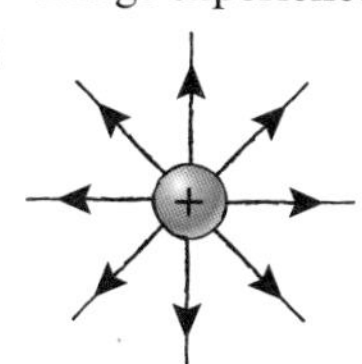

Radial field with arrows pointing outwards **(1)**

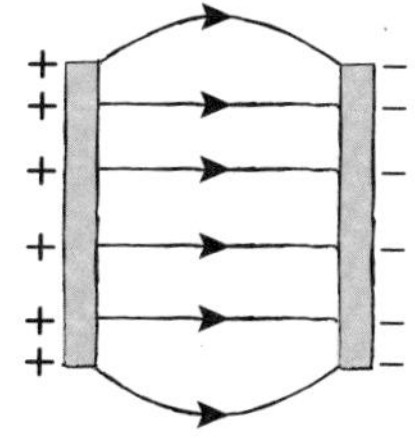

Parallel lines and arrows from + to – **(1)** (ignore curved lines)

3. (a) Apply friction/rub the balloon with the cloth **(1)**. Electrons transfer to the balloon. **(1)** Electrons are negative. **(1)**

(b) The – charge on the balloon repels the – charge in the hair/attracts the + charge in the hair. **(1)** A + charge is induced in the hair. **(1)** This + charge is then attracted towards the negatively charged balloon/opposite charges attract. **(1)**

4. The smoke particles are given a negative charge from the grid. **(1)** They experience a non-contact force in the positive electric fields of the plates **(1)** so they accelerate towards/are attracted to the positively charged plates. **(1)** They are then knocked off the plates and collected in the trap. **(1)**

58–61. Specific heat capacity and specific latent heat

1. (a) $\Delta Q = m \times c \times \Delta\theta$

$24\,000 = 0.35 \times c \times 15$ **(1)**

$c = \frac{24\,000}{5.25}$ **(1)** = 4600 J/kg °C **(1)**

(b) Reduce energy loss to the surroundings using better insulation **(1)** so the energy measured is the energy used to heat up the water **(1)**.

(c) $\Delta Q = m \times c \times \Delta\theta$

$\Delta Q = 0.35 \times 4600 \times 8$ **(1)**

$\Delta Q = 13\,000$ J **(1)**

2. (a)

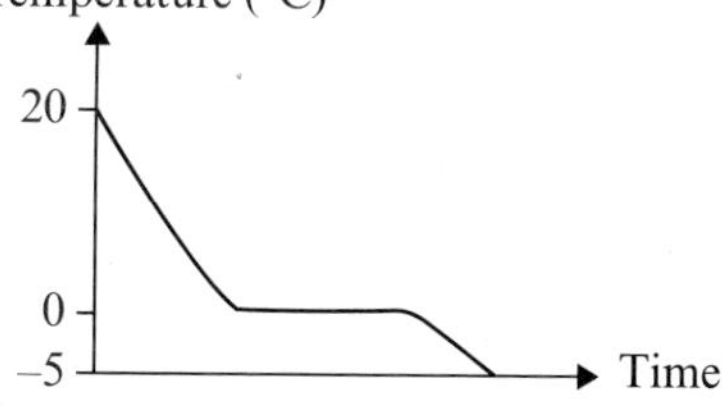

Line drops from 20 on *y*-axis, then levels off at 0 **(1)**; line remains level for a time, then drops again to −5 **(1)**

(b) The specific latent heat of fusion is the energy that must be transferred to 1 kg of a substance to change its state between a solid and a liquid. **(1)**

(c) $Q = m \times L$

$Q = 0.15 \times 334\,000$ **(1)** = 50 100 J **(1)**

62–65. Pressure

1. (a) $P = \frac{F}{A}$ and pressure on X = pressure on pad

$\frac{104}{8} = \frac{F}{25}$ **(1)**

$F = \frac{104 \times 25}{8}$ **(1)**

$F = 325$ N **(1)**

(b) $E = F \times d$

work done by piston X = work done by **both** brake pad pistons

work done by piston X
$= 104 \times 0.0675 = 7.02\,\text{J}$ **(1)**

work done by one brake pad piston
$= \frac{7.02}{2} = 3.51\,\text{J}$ **(1)**

$325 \times d = 3.51$ **(1)**

$d = \frac{3.51}{325} = 0.0108\,\text{m}$ **(1)**

2. (a) The pressure exerted by liquid 1 is greater than the pressure exerted by liquid 2 **(1)** from the same height **(1)** so liquid 1 has a higher density **(1)**.

(b) $P = h \times \rho \times g$

$4450 = 0.5 \times \rho \times 10$ **(1)**

$\rho = \frac{4450}{0.5 \times 10}$ **(1)**

$\rho = 890\,\text{kg/m}^3$ **(1)**

3. $P_1 \times V_1 = P_2 \times V_2$

$100\,000 \times V_1 = 220\,000 \times 0.0025$ **(1)**

$V_1 = \frac{220\,000 \times 0.0025}{100\,000}$ **(1)**

$V_1 = 0.0055\,\text{m}^3$ **(1)**

Formula sheet

In your exam you will be provided with the following list of equations. You will need to learn the equations that are not on the formula sheet. Equations in red font aren't required for Pearson Edexcel GCSE (9–1) Combined Science Higher.

Equations

(final velocity)^2 – (initial velocity)^2 = 2 × acceleration × distance $v^2 - u^2 = 2 \times a \times x$
force = change in momentum ÷ time $F = \frac{(mv - mu)}{t}$
energy transferred = current × potential difference × time $E = I \times V \times t$
force on a conductor at right angles to a magnetic field carrying a current = magnetic flux density × current × length $F = B \times I \times l$
$\frac{\text{voltage across primary coil}}{\text{voltage across secondary coil}} = \frac{\text{number of turns in primary coil}}{\text{number of turns in secondary coil}}$ $\frac{V_p}{V_s} = \frac{N_p}{N_s}$
potential difference across primary coil × current in primary coil = potential difference across secondary coil × current in secondary coil $V_p \times I_p = V_s \times I_s$
change in thermal energy = mass × specific heat capacity × change in temperature $\Delta Q = m \times c \times \Delta\theta$
thermal energy for a change of state = mass × specific latent heat $Q = m \times L$
$P_1 V_1 = P_2 V_2$ to calculate pressure or volume for gases of fixed mass at constant temperature
energy transferred in stretching = 0.5 × spring constant × (extension)^2 $E = \frac{1}{2} \times k \times x^2$
pressure due to a column of liquid = height of column × density of liquid × gravitational field strength $P = h \times \rho \times g$

Match to the Revise Pearson Edexcel GCSE (9–1) Combined Science Higher Revision Guide

If you are taking the Pearson Edexcel GCSE (9–1) Combined Science Higher exam, use the table below to match the pages and knowledge check questions to the Revise Pearson Edexcel GCSE (9–1) Combined Science Higher Revision Guide. The circled knowledge check questions are Pearson Edexcel GCSE (9–1) Physics Higher only questions.

Knowledge Check question	Nail It! Physics	Combined Science Higher RG pages
1, 2, 3	6–9	167–170
4	10–13	172–173, 175–176
5		174
6	14–17	177, 178
7		180
8, (9), (10)	30–33	191
11	26–29	194, 196
12		200
13, 14		201
15		206
16	42–45	203, 207–209
(17), (18)		
19	18–21	215–217
(20), (21)	22–25	
22		219
23, 24		221
	34–37	186, 213
	38–41	203–205, 210–211
25, 26	46–49	223, 228
27		229
(28), (29), (30)	54–57	
31	50–53	237–238
32	58–61	240, 243–244
(33)	62–65	

Notes

Notes

Notes

Published by Pearson Education Limited, 80 Strand, London, WC2R 0RL.

www.pearsonschoolsandfecolleges.co.uk

Copies of official specifications for all Pearson qualifications may be found on the website: qualifications.pearson.com

Typeset and illustrated by Newgen KnowledgeWorks Pvt. Ltd., Chennai, India
Produced by Newgen Publishing UK
Cover illustration by © Miriam Sturdee

First published 2020

23 22 21 20
10 9 8 7 6 5 4 3 2 1

British Library Cataloguing in Publication Data
A catalogue record for this book is available from the British Library

ISBN 978 1 292 29429 2

Printed in Slovakia by Neografia

Note from the publisher

1. While the publishers have made every attempt to ensure that advice on the qualification and its assessment is accurate, the official specification and associated assessment guidance materials are the only authoritative source of information and should always be referred to for definitive guidance.

Pearson examiners have not contributed to any sections in this resource relevant to examination papers for which they have responsibility.

2. Pearson has robust editorial processes, including answer and fact checks, to ensure the accuracy of the content in this publication, and every effort is made to ensure this publication is free of errors. We are, however, only human, and occasionally errors do occur. Pearson is not liable for any misunderstandings that arise as a result of errors in this publication, but it is our priority to ensure that the content is accurate. If you spot an error, please do contact us at resourcescorrections@pearson.com so we can make sure it is corrected.